Here Is Real Magic

Here Is Real Magic

*A Magician's Search for Wonder
in the Modern World*

Nate Staniforth

BLOOMSBURY

NEW YORK · LONDON · OXFORD · NEW DELHI · SYDNEY

Bloomsbury USA
An imprint of Bloomsbury Publishing Plc

1385 Broadway
New York
NY 10018
USA

50 Bedford Square
London
WC1B 3DP
UK

www.bloomsbury.com

BLOOMSBURY and the Diana logo are trademarks of Bloomsbury Publishing Plc

First published 2018

Author's note: To write this book I drew upon my journal from India, my own memory of the events and places, and Andy's extensive video footage from our trip. Much of the dialog in the second half of the book comes directly from those transcripts, though in some instances I had to reconstruct dialog when no record of the conversation existed. In those cases I have attempted to consult those involved to ensure the conversation has been represented accurately. Some of the names in this book have been changed to preserve anonymity.

ISBN: HB: 978-1-63286-424-6
           ePub: 978-1-63286-426-0

LIBRARY OF CONGRESS CATALOGING-IN-PUBLICATION DATA

Names: Staniforth, Nate, author.
Title: Here is real magic / Nate Staniforth.
Description: New York: Bloomsbury, 2018.
Identifiers: LCCN 2017016409 | ISBN 9781632864246 (hardcover: acid-free paper)
Subjects: LCSH: Staniforth, Nate. | Magicians—United States—Biography.
Classification: LCC GV1545.S77 A3 2018 | DDC 793.8092 [B]—dc23
LC record available at https://lccn.loc.gov/2017016409

2 4 6 8 10 9 7 5 3 1

Typeset by Westchester Publishing Services
Printed and bound in the U.S.A. by Berryville Graphics Inc., Berryville, Virginia

To find out more about our authors and books visit www.bloomsbury.com. Here you will find extracts, author interviews, details of forthcoming events and the option to sign up for our newsletters.

Bloomsbury books may be purchased for business or promotional use. For information on bulk purchases please contact Macmillan Corporate and Premium Sales Department at specialmarkets@macmillan.com.

To the Magicians

Above all, watch with glittering eyes the whole world around you because the greatest secrets are always hidden in the most unlikely places. Those who don't believe in magic will never find it.

—*Roald Dahl*

CONTENTS

INTRODUCTION

I'M TWO WEEKS into a three-month tour and tonight I'm at a college in Chicago, performing a show at an on-campus bar in the basement of the student union. Three hundred people are packed into a space that should hold only half that many. The room is dark and noisy. The audience is on its way to being drunk—even very drunk—and while this may not be the worst performance environment I have ever faced, it's close.

In a gamble to take charge of the situation I've abandoned the small pipe-and-drape platform in the corner and now I'm standing on a table in the middle of the room. Every audience is different. Sometimes you have to charm them or cajole them, sometimes you have to entice or fascinate, and sometimes you have to roll up your sleeves and fight, winning the room with a careful blend of intensity and goodwill, convincing the audience that you're either a genius or a madman and that, either way, they should probably stop for a second and listen. Tonight my arrival onstage was met with a mixture of applause and disdain, the audience being equal parts people who came to see a magic show and people who came to drink. One six-foot, two-hundred-fifty-pound bruiser with a crew cut started booing even before they finished reading my introduction. Now I am standing on his table.

Except it's not really me up there. The version of me who's capable of climbing up in front of a few hundred people and commanding the room is tougher and smarter than I am. He is wild and unpredictable. He's faster on his feet and capable of making bold, intuitive leaps that I could never make in the real world, and he can stick the landing, too. He's also kind of an asshole. He cares far more about the show than he does the sensibilities of the audience, and his priorities can get me into trouble.

"Listen," I say, scanning the room, deliberately meeting the eyes of everyone who booed just a minute ago, "in a minute, you are going to see something impossible. Some of you are going to scream. Some of you are going to yell. This gentleman here is going to shit himself." Crew Cut is looking at me like he wants to fight, but I have him pinned in his seat with the gaze of three hundred people who are finally paying attention. For the moment he can only glower.

"I'm not doing this for the money. I'm not doing this for the glory. If I were, I sure as hell wouldn't be here. I'm here because I've spent my entire life learning to do something incredible, and tonight I'm going to share it with you. When I'm done, you can clap, you can boo, you can stay, you can leave—I don't give a shit."

This succeeds in shocking them. I've pushed the audience about as far as they will go and I can feel their attention wavering between fascination and offense. Now the entire room has turned to watch. Whether this is because they're interested in seeing what I'm about to do or because they think I'm about to get the shit kicked out of me doesn't matter. For the moment, I have them.

"I'm going to give this gentleman my wallet. He probably hates me right now, so I understand this might seem dangerous, but I'm choosing him because he's the biggest one in the bar, and I need someone to keep the wallet safe." I'm edging back the hostility now. At some point I need these people to like me, so now that I have their attention I'm dialing down the aggression.

I look down at Crew Cut. "What's your name?"

He looks at me like he wishes he'd gone somewhere else for the evening.

"Marcus."

I hand him my wallet. "Marcus, I want you to put this on the table and put both hands on top of it. Don't open it yet. But make sure that no one else opens it either. Got it?"

Marcus nods. I've put him on the spot but I'm about to make it up to him. I know that if this works he will remember this experience for the rest of his life. He will tell his children about this moment. I've spent six years developing this illusion and it's been worth the effort. If I had five minutes to justify my entire existence as a magician, this is what I would perform. Given my strained relationship with tonight's audience, five minutes might be all I have left.

I turn to the rest of the room.

"I'm going to need six random people to help. If I just asked for volunteers you might think that I had confederates in the audience, so I'm going to take this gentleman's hat"—and here I reach down and snatch a baseball cap from someone's head— "and throw it out into the room. If you catch it, stand up. We'll do that six times."

Thirty seconds later six people are standing and the man has his hat back.

"I need each of you to think of a number between one and fifty. When I point to you, call your number out loud so everyone can hear."

"Sixteen."

"Thirty-two."

"Nine."

"Forty-three."

"Eleven."

I pause before the last person. A girl is standing in the back of the room, holding a beer in one hand. I don't think she came here intending to watch a magic show, but she started paying attention as soon as I climbed onto the table, and when the hat flew toward her a minute ago she jumped up to catch it.

"What's your name?"

"Jessica."

"Jessica, before you tell me your number I just want to say this: When you go home tonight, you are going to be unable to sleep. You're going to lie in bed, staring at the ceiling, driving yourself crazy wondering what would have happened if you had named a number other than the number you are about to name."

The audience laughs. Jessica just listens.

"Before you give me your number, I want you to know in your heart of hearts that it was a free choice, that there is no way I could have gotten inside your head to make you give me the number I wanted. Right?"

She nods slowly.

"What number are you thinking of?"

"Fourteen."

Silence here. Every great illusion has a moment of calm before the build to the end, and right now the room is completely quiet. At some point in the last minute the bartender started watching and turned off the music. Everyone is still.

"Some of you are going to think of this as a trick, and that's fine. I'm a magician, and magicians do tricks. But we can all agree that up to this point there is no way I could have controlled which of you were going to catch the baseball hat or what numbers you would say."

The six people nod.

"Some of you are going to think of this as a coincidence, but I want to point out that the odds of this working by chance alone are in the trillions. What are the numbers again? Sixteen, thirty-two, nine, forty-three, eleven, and fourteen, right? Look at this."

Marcus has been sitting at the table the entire time, holding the wallet and watching the performance. I point to the wallet.

"Marcus, could you stand up for a second?"

He stands. I ask him to hold the wallet up above his head so everyone can see, and he does.

"You have been holding my wallet the entire time. Open it and look inside. You should find a lottery ticket. Take it out."

Marcus opens the wallet and removes the lottery ticket.

"This isn't a winning lottery ticket. I'm not a millionaire. But I want you to look at the numbers on the lottery ticket. I'm going to hand you the microphone. Read them out loud."

I am watching his face now, waiting for him to see it.

There.

"Oh," he says quietly. "Oh shit. Oh no." He looks at me. His eyes are very wide. He looks back at the lottery ticket. "Oh shit. Shit. Shit. Shit. Shit."

He has been holding the microphone. Everyone else is straining for a view of whatever it is that he's seeing, but they can hear him clearly.

"Oh holy shit. No fucking way. Get the fuck out of here, man. What the fuck?" The audience is watching Marcus ascend to a sort of crazed delirium.

"Read them the numbers printed on the ticket, Marcus."

Marcus raises the microphone. "Sixteen, thirty-two, nine, forty-three, eleven, and fourteen."

The room explodes. I don't know how else to say it. One moment three hundred people are leaning forward in a dead quiet, straining to understand what's happened. Then Marcus reads the numbers and panic surges through the room as if a fire is breaking out. People are on their feet, screaming and jumping and turning to one another. Some are laughing. Someone runs for the exit, knocking over a table. Jessica has her hands on her face, her mouth open. Marcus has dropped the microphone. He is reading the ticket over and over again, shaking his head and laughing.

I want you to see his face. I want you to see the joy, the open, unaffected joy. It's the kind of joy that reminds you that what you mistook for dull, uninspired brutishness a moment before was actually just weight—the weight of worry, of pain, of anxiety, of the world—and for a moment it has gone, and the face that shines without it is extraordinary. Magicians get to see people at their very best, and in this transformation you can see actual magic through the illusion.

As if on cue, the bartender restarts the music. I have been onstage for five minutes. I don't remember what happens for the rest of the show and it doesn't matter. For the moment I'm filled with adrenaline and warm from victory. I am wide awake. Tomorrow I'll leave early and travel all day so I can do it all over again in another town for another audience, but right now my thoughts are here in this room, and the room before that, and the hundreds and hundreds of theaters, auditoriums, and ballrooms before that, all the way back to my first performance. I was nine years old. I made a coin vanish on the playground, the entire world went crazy, and I learned that you can say something with a magic trick that is hard to say any other way.

PART ONE

ALCHEMY

SOMEWHERE IN MY parents' house there's a picture of me at age seven. I'm crouched in the grass in the backyard on a summer evening, surrounded by fireflies, lifting my cupped hands as if I'm holding a secret and want to share it. At that age it's easy to be amazed. The world is new and you are new in it and free from the ridiculous certainty that comes so easily with age that the inner workings of the universe are not only knowable but already known.

My first interest in magic came long before I became a magician, and though I have gone on to perform my show thousands of times for hundreds of thousands of people, to this day when I think about magic I think about two memories from a time before I knew anything about tricks.

The first was when I lay on the floor under the piano when my dad played before bedtime. During the day he worked as a dentist, but we rarely saw him at the office. We saw him when he came home and painted in the basement or paced the backyard with a yellow legal pad writing terse, fiery letters to the editor of the local paper about public policy and the environment. He'd read them to us at dinner and my mom would invariably protest—"Art! You can't say that in public!"—and my younger brother and I would laugh in delight at her exasperation. But in the evenings he would turn out the lights and sit at the piano and I would lie underneath, listening. The only light in the room came from the lamp for the sheet music—Beethoven, Bach, Rachmaninoff. The music filled the house but from underneath I could hear the mechanics of the piano, too—the faint creak of the pedals, the click of the keys, the felted hammers striking the strings, the deep resonance of the sounding board. You could get lost in those sounds.

From the most expensive concert grand to the cheapest church basement clunker, a piano is essentially a wooden box stretched with wire. It's a cumbersome piece of furniture. And as I listened all those nights before bed, I realized that the majesty and the mystery of the piano is that this heavy, ungainly apparatus can give birth to the *Moonlight Sonata*. That you can coax from this box of wood and wire a sound so light and pure and beautiful, that anything so firmly rooted in the physical could call into being something that borders so closely on the transcendent: this—lying on the floor underneath my dad's piano—was the first time I really noticed the experience of magic.

The second came maybe a year or so later. One night my mom came upstairs to wake me and my younger brother. It felt like midnight but it was probably only nine or ten. She held my sleeping baby sister and asked us to come downstairs. Dad had already started the car and put blankets on the back bench seat and we set out into the night, on an adventure, they said.

We lived in Ames, Iowa—a small liberal college town surrounded by endless stretches of corn and soybean fields—and fifteen minutes out of town on the two-lane highway we were beyond the reach of the city's light and enveloped in total darkness. The entire world was reduced to the faint illumination of the dashboard and a short smudge of yellow from the headlights on the road ahead. We pulled off the highway onto a gravel road. Dad turned off the engine and we all got out.

On either side of the road the corn rose above my head and the warm summer wind breathed quietly through the stalks. I stood there, expectant, I imagine, and uncertain why we had come. And then I looked up.

This was not the sky. I had seen the sky—I knew how the sky looked at night, and this was some different thing entirely. The comforting veil of faint stars that mildly wrapped every other night had been replaced by a void of terrible space and time and distance, stretching infinitely up and infinitely away, forever. There was Mars. There was the Milky Way. There was the universe in all of its awful, overpowering majesty towering above us, inexplicably high and distant, hostile and beckoning, dangerous and wild, a haunted place where we were the only ghosts for miles.

Then the meteor shower began. My dad led us up a low hill and laid the blankets on the wet grass. I don't remember how long we all lay there, watching the sky, but I became aware for the first time that the entire planet—the oceans, London, Mount Everest, everything—lay directly and totally behind me. Somehow the night sky had unveiled the true nature of this road, mistaken during the day as a gravel route through a cornfield but revealed now as the final patch of earth at the very edge of the world. That night the mystery of our situation felt like one grand miracle, hidden just out of sight unless you really try to see it. That there is something rather than nothing, and that we are here to be part of it—surely this is amazing. How is this so easy to forget? How is this so easy to ignore, silence, or overlook in the pursuit of other things? Even at a young age we learn the universe is filled with loneliness and fear, but lying there, clinging to the blanket as the earth spun and the meteors fell and the whole of existence stood out on display, I recognized that whatever else it was and whatever I became in it, the universe was also filled—to the very cusp—with wonder.

Now, decades later, I worry that the experience of wonder becomes harder and harder for me to find as I get older. This has nothing to do with education—wonder is not the product of ignorance—but it does have something to do with certainty. As an adult, I am tempted to establish and reaffirm at all times the boundaries of my existence—to say "This is my life and I have a good grip on it," like an ostrich in his own personal kingdom under the sand. But my favorite moments are the ones that shoot this certainty full of holes, that barge in unannounced and track mud all over the carpets, grab me by the shirt, drag me out into the street and say, in effect, "Wake up, you fool, and open your eyes. There is more to it than that."

So if I were to tell you about my experience as a human being I wouldn't tell you about my triumphs or my defeats. Everyone has them, and they're more the result of life than the actual stuff of its creation. I wouldn't tell you about my fears or my suffering. Again, everyone has them, and mine are not particularly unique or acute. All things considered, so far I have been pretty lucky.

Instead, I would tell you about the moments I have stood rapt in awe, or quiet with wonder, and in so doing, seen beyond the surface of things. I have spent most of my life and all of my career trying to understand this experience, yet it has never become commonplace or ordinary. On the contrary, it stands out as one of the only experiences in this world that is wholly good. Wonder, astonishment, magic—that sense of waking up and seeing things the way you saw them before they became ordinary. This is the root of it for me, the curious joy and the primal dread of the unknown. There's something there— in the dark sky at night or in the bare branches of the trees against the gray November clouds, or in the summer wind as it comes in from the sea with the smell of another land just over the horizon—reminding us that the universe, the world, and the human heart are larger and more mysterious than we can possibly imagine. This is magic.

So this—all of this—came first. The magic tricks came later, and the less we dwell on them, the better. This is not a book about tricks. This is a book about magic—the experience of magic—and you can find it anywhere. People find it in music and movies, in mountaintops or conversation, in the night sky or in the *Moonlight Sonata*. Magic tricks are just a way to remember something you already know, or maybe knew and then forgot somewhere along the way. Take them for what they are and they're nothing. You can't look at them. You have to look through them, like a telescope.

I BECAME A magician by accident.

When I was nine years old I learned how to make a coin disappear. I'd read *The Lord of the Rings* and ventured into the adult section of the library to search for a book of spells—nine being that curious age at which you're old enough to work through thirteen hundred pages of arcane fantasy literature but young enough to still hold out hope that you might find a book of real, actual magic in the library. The book I found instead taught basic sleight of hand technique, and I dedicated the next months to practice.

At first the magic wasn't any good. At first it wasn't even magic, it was just a trick, and at first it was just a bad trick. I spent hours of each day in the bathroom, running through the secret moves in front of the mirror above the sink and getting lost in the possibility that if I became good enough I could make the coin disappear. I dropped the coin over and over, a thousand times in a day, and after two weeks of this my mom got a carpet sample from the hardware store and placed it under the mirror to muffle the sound of the coin falling again and again to the floor. I had heard my dad work through passages of new music on the piano, so I knew how to practice—slowly, deliberately, going for precision rather than speed—and one day I tried the illusion in the mirror and the coin vanished. It did not look like a magic trick. It looked like a miracle.

One of the lessons you learn very early on as a magician is that the most amazing part of a magic trick has nothing to do with the secret. The secret is simple and often dull: a hidden piece of tape, a small mirror, a duplicate playing card. In this case the secret was a series of covert maneuvers to hide the coin behind my hand in the act of opening it, a dance of the fingers that I learned so completely I didn't even have to think. I would close my hand, open it, and the coin would vanish not by skill but by real magic.

One day I made the coin vanish on the playground. We had been playing football and were standing by the backstop in the field behind the school. A dozen people were watching. I showed the coin to everyone. Then it disappeared.

Imagine for a moment that you are at school. You see someone holding a quarter. Then, without warning or context, the quarter disappears. Or imagine that you see anything that would qualify as impossible. A man walks through a wall. A garbage can levitates. The pages in your hand turn into a pigeon and fly away. This would not be a small experience. It would, in fact, be one of the defining moments of your life. Your instinct would not be to applaud or laugh or turn jovially to the person next to you on the train and offer an explanation as to how your book could have disappeared. It would not feel like a piece of entertainment—it would feel like a car crash or an explosion, or a violation of the laws of nature and a direct, crippling assault on your fundamental sense of certainty about the ways of the world. The appropriate response to something that feels truly impossible is not applause: the appropriate response is fear; fear and, as you are running away, some hidden, pure, secret joy that maybe the world is bigger than you thought.

In any case, they screamed. They yelled, laughed, scrambled away. Everyone went crazy. This was great. This was Bilbo Baggins from *The Lord of the Rings* terrifying the guests at his birthday party by putting the One Ring on his finger and just vanishing in front of everyone.

The teacher on duty crossed the playground to investigate. Mrs. Tanner was a wiry, vengeful woman who dominated her classroom with an appetite for humiliation and an oversized plastic golf club she wielded like a weapon, slamming it down on the desks of the unruly and uncommitted. Once she swung it directly at Aaron Gray, stopping the head of the club just a few inches from his face, which dissolved immediately into a crumpled mess of tears and shrieking, sobbing fear. Aaron Grey was a bastard, to be sure, but Mrs. Tanner was worse.

She marched toward me and demanded to know what was going on. The coin vanished for her, too. She stopped. "Do it again," she said, and I did. I'm sure my hands were shaking, but when I looked up everything had changed. This was someone else entirely. It's possible that Mrs. Tanner didn't jump up and down and scream with quite as much volume as the third graders, but I will remember the look on her face—the look of wide-eyed, open-mouthed wonder—forever.

Two certainties. First, this was clearly the greatest thing in the world. I had never seen anyone react to anything the way my teacher had responded when the coin disappeared. I kept seeing her face—the stern, authoritarian façade melting into shock, fear, elation, and joy, all at once. The kids, too. The same new kids at the same new school had been transformed for a moment from a vaguely indifferent, vaguely hostile pack of scavengers and carnivores into real people. If you could make people feel like this, why wouldn't you do it all the time? Why didn't everyone do this? For anyone—but especially for a nine-year-old boy at a new school—this transformation is almost indistinguishable from real magic.

The second certainty was harder to reconcile. I had uncovered a mystery. The more I thought about it, the stranger it became, and even now it intrigues me as much as it did that day on the playground.

Here it is: all of it—the chaos, the shouting, the wide-eyed wonder—all of this came from a coin trick. As amazing as it was for my audience, the moment was far more amazing for me. I knew that it was just a trick and I was just a kid. But the reactions of the students and the teacher were so much greater than the sum of these modest parts that I didn't know how to explain them. I was back under the piano again, hearing the creaking and straining of the instrument bringing out a sound that was maybe from that piece of furniture but certainly not of it. The weight of this disparity is hard to overemphasize. Something incredible had happened that day on the playground. I might have caused it, but it had not come from me. I had inadvertently tapped into something visceral and wild. I could still see the teacher's face. I could still hear the shouts of fear, astonishment, and joy. The joy was the hardest to explain. Surprise comes easy, but joy never does. I was an alchemist who had somehow— unknowingly, unintentionally—discovered how to turn lead into gold.

Even a nine-year-old knows this is impossible. You could only do that with real magic.

~

I BECAME A magician because I loved the experience of awe and wonder. Also because I thought a good magic trick might impress girls, frighten bullies, stupefy adults, and generally lead to a life of mystery and adventure. When the coin vanished on the playground I felt as if I had found a secret path into another world and I wanted to see where it led.

The Ames Public Library was my only real link to the world of magic, and there I uncovered the secret architecture of deception invented by magicians to create marvels. I learned everything I could find: technique, theory, sleight of hand, misdirection. Of the many misconceptions the general public holds about the world of magicians, the belief that we are particularly good at keeping secrets is the most baffling. Even a modestly funded public library contains entire lifetimes of material—how to find a chosen card, how to pick a lock, how to levitate a dollar bill, and on and on—and for a child these discoveries do not feel like magic tricks. They feel like a hidden map to buried treasure or a letter that falls down your chimney on your eleventh birthday that says *Dear Harry, you are a wizard.* Here in these books of magic the impossible became possible and the world of fiction was suddenly and unexpectedly made real.

From the beginning I could see that behind the deceptions in each of the magic tricks lurked something very real—larger, but harder to see. Even though the tricks were ostensibly "fake," the experience of the audience was genuine, palpable, and more than a little unsettling. The young magician discovers the disarming ease with which a good piece of magic can open a window to something raw and untamed within the human spirit that is usually kept private and shielded from the public view.

I remember doing magic for a friend of my parents one afternoon—a burly, gregarious man from Chicago who liked to slap you on the back and grinned as though everything was an inside joke. He started watching politely, face frozen in that vanilla-frosting smile adults reserve for children when they want to communicate just how completely they are paying attention, but then the magic happened and all of that dropped away. "Holy shit!" he shrieked. "Holy shit! Art, did you see that?" He looked at my dad, and then down at me again, his face a rapture of unbridled joy and incredulity. "Holy shit!"

What strange current passes through the mind of a grown man as he jumps up and down in the kitchen shouting "Holy shit!" at a ten-year-old boy whose magic trick requires nothing more than a duplicate playing card and a piece of double-sided tape? Certainly this was a clue to something essential. You can only see so many grown, sober, educated adults jumping up and out of themselves with amazement before you begin to suspect that the magician is tapping into something primal, even universal, that goes far deeper than anything gained or lost through age and experience. Everyone assumes that magic is best appreciated by children, but any magician in the world will tell you that while you might be hired at the birthday party to entertain the kids, it's the adults watching from the back of the room who react with the most depth and emotion.

A YEAR OR so later, David Copperfield—the most famous magician in the world—brought his international tour to Ames, Iowa, and my fate was sealed. I still remember coming home from school with my brother one day that fall. The house felt different. My mom appeared, smiling in the doorway, and before we even dropped our backpacks to the floor she said, "Do you know what I did today?" Clearly, it was something wonderful. "Do you know who is coming to town? David Copperfield is performing at C. Y. Stephens Auditorium and we're all going to go. I got tickets today and we're in the third row."

She dropped to her knee and handed me a newspaper clipping showing a man standing astride a motorcycle on a stage filled with light and smoke. DAVID COPPERFIELD—BEYOND IMAGINATION—LIVE ON STAGE.

I knew about David Copperfield somehow, though at this point I had still never actually seen a magician. Ames doesn't get a lot of magic shows, and I hadn't seen any of the TV specials, so my only knowledge about how it should look came from books. And now the biggest magic show on the planet was coming to a theater just down the road.

The night of the show I'd insisted that we arrive at the theater early to make sure we had plenty of time to be excited in our seats before the show began. My brother and I had dressed up for the occasion—one of the two or three times in my entire childhood that I wasn't wearing sweatpants—and my parents parked the car and walked us toward the towering, monolithic C. Y. Stephens Auditorium. It rose from the parking lot like a mountain, the tallest building in town. A line stretched around the theater and in the back we saw three semi trucks with COPPERFIELD spelled out along the side. All day at school we had been talking about the show. Apparently that Sunday the youth pastor at one of the churches in town had condemned magic as the work of the devil, infusing my fourth-grade classroom with controversy, and someone at my dad's office who had seen the show in Chicago a month before wasn't allowing her children to go because she feared the magic would frighten them. My parents thought we could handle it, but before the show they talked to my brother and me about everything we would see—specifically, that these were illusions performed by a magician and we didn't need to worry. I clutched my ticket and handed it to the man at the door. Then we went in.

As we found our seats, I looked around the room. It was full, and, surprisingly, full of adults. My brother and I were maybe the youngest ones there. This was not children's night at the theater. The sound system blasted something modern and loud and smoke filled the darkened stage and billowed out into the cavernous hall, catching the overhead houselights and transforming this auditorium into someplace strange and vaguely ominous. The room crackled, as if a spark would set off the whole thing. Even before the start of the show this was the greatest night of my life. I was ten years old and living in the middle of the cornfields, and the most famous magician in the world was about to walk out onto that stage and blow the whole city away.

I don't remember the show. The specifics don't matter. Amazing things happened and at the end we all stood and clapped for a long, long time. At some point during the performance I remember looking over at my parents. They looked like children. These were no longer adults. Whatever time and age had put upon them was gone. I had never seen my dad smile like that before, like a kid at a magic show.

When the applause finally ended I didn't want to leave. I wanted to stay in my seat. I wanted to live there and feel that way again and again. If you could use your life to give people the experience we'd just had at the show, why would you do anything else? Children can want something with more keening power than anyone, and in this moment—and all of the ones that followed—I wanted to do magic above all else. Take everything else but leave me this. I will give anything.

HEROES

THE HISTORY OF magic is an improbable lineage of grand masters, rebels, rejects, thieves, traitors, geniuses, and inventors, and before long I had found an entirely new set of heroes. Magic draws people in from all levels of society—the list of great magicians throughout history includes impoverished immigrants and royalty—and their stories were larger than life, filled with mystery, adventure, and courage. In Ames, Iowa, the prospect of becoming a professional magician was as exotic and unlikely as becoming a pirate, and so to me, these magicians weren't mere entertainers so much as valiant knights who fought back against whatever it is in the world that dampens the fire and spoils the dreams of lesser men. Somehow they had broken free of the invisible weight that drags the gaze of the aspiring astronomer or poet down from the heavens and fixes it on another— safer—line of work. I'd sit on the floor of the library between the shelves with Melbourne Christopher's *Illustrated History of Magic* and James Randi's *Conjuring* open beside me and read about these emissaries from another world where magic was real and anything was possible.

I learned about Blackstone—the cabinet-maker-turned-illusionist who invented one of the greatest illusions of the twentieth century. He strode to the front of the stage, stripped off his coat, rolled his sleeves to his elbows, and displayed a simple white lightbulb. The stage lights dimmed slightly. For a moment, nothing happened. Then the lightbulb began to glow.

Today, in an age when we have batteries the size of aspirin, this would not amaze anyone. In the 1920s, when the smallest battery was the size of a saltshaker and far too large to conceal inside a lightbulb, the sight of a bare, unconnected lightbulb illuminated at the fingertips was a headline-grabbing, show-stopping sensation. But this was just the beginning.

On Blackstone's command, the lightbulb began to float. It rose from his hands and levitated from one end of the stage to the other—through a hoop to dispel the notion of threads—and then out over the heads of the audience. Slowly, silently, the single glowing lightbulb glided eerily through the cavernous theater. It was a sensation.

Blackstone wasn't alone. I learned about Jean-Eugène Robert-Houdin, the French watchmaker who became a celebrated magician in Paris before the French government sent him to suppress an uprising in Algeria. The revolt was incited by a quasireligious group who passed off sleight-of-hand magic as actual miraculous power to assert their authority, and in 1856 Emperor Louis-Napoleon commanded Robert-Houdin to perform his most amazing feats for the leaders of the tribe. Robert-Houdin was ordered to demonstrate the superiority of French magic—and, by proxy, French rule—making him perhaps the first magician since Merlin to be sent into battle to subdue an enemy with magic.

I learned about Carter the Great, the Ohio farm boy who became a real-life Indiana Jones and barnstormed his way around the world at the turn of the century, fleeing from bandits and searching the globe for great illusions as he traveled from continent to continent with his elaborate stage show. I learned about Thurston, Kellar, Dante—the history of magic is filled with stories of great magicians and the impossible feats they invented, and I devoured everything I could find.

But mostly I learned about Houdini.

Today, a child sitting on the floor between the shelves in the library is far better equipped to see Houdini as he really was than is any modern adult. For a theater audience in 1899—or a young person today—the Magician-in-Tuxedo was not a cliché. For them, the figure of the Magician stood not at the ostracized periphery of popular culture but instead much closer to the center. In the age before movies or television or the Internet, an audience seeking marvels went to a magic show, and Houdini was the king of magicians. He toured the United States, the UK, Europe, Russia, and Australia, and everywhere he went Houdini created a sensation.

In 1900, the twenty-six-year-old Houdini and his wife, Bess, traveled to Great Britain hoping to find work in the West End theater district. With no contract and no referral from an American theater, Houdini set out to impress the London theater elite with an escape from the most famous police force in the world, Scotland Yard. I could picture him—short and athletic, like a boxer, wiry hair standing on end and his black frock coat blowing out behind him as he marched down the Victoria Embankment. The story goes that he stormed into police headquarters to proclaim that he was the great Harry Houdini, the very man himself, and could escape from anything in the world. Scotland Yard superintendent William Melville overheard this boast and immediately dragged him out into the street, pulled his arms around a pillar, and snapped a pair of handcuffs around his wrists. "This is how we treat Yanks who come over here and get themselves into trouble," he said, and promised to return after lunch to set him free. As he turned to walk away, Melville heard the handcuffs clatter to the pavement. "Wait a minute," Houdini said, falling into stride next to the astonished superintendent. "I'll join you."

In 1907, one hundred thousand workingmen and women of New York abandoned their posts in factories, shops, banks, and offices and flooded the streets to watch a straitjacketed Houdini dangle upside down on a rope suspended from a crane one hundred feet above Forty-Sixth Street. He swung back and forth, trying to leverage his body free of the jacket, and the arc of his swing grew wider and wider until he crashed through an office window, sending shards of glass glittering to the pavement below. But he escaped anyway. First one hand emerged. Then the other. Then he was free.

Houdini could escape from anything, certainly, but his greatest feat was making those feats resonate with a strength and a power far beyond the simple mechanics of release. Don't think of Houdini as a magician. Think of Houdini as the original Bruce Springsteen—an artist who rose to international superstardom as a living, breathing metaphor of the daily struggles of the working class. Houdini was the son of impoverished immigrants from Hungary. For a generation of other immigrants facing the daunting task of beginning a new life in a new country—or for a ten-year-old boy in our time trying to begin his own—Houdini stood as a glorious example of someone who set out to do the impossible and actually did it.

I read everything I could find about Houdini. At some point I acquired a highlighter and, with a dim understanding that its purpose was to mark important passages so I could come back to them later for further study, highlighted an entire biography. When I was done, the whole book was yellow. Every word. It was all important to me.

~

HOUDINI DIED IN 1926, making way for David Berglas—the International Man of Mystery—who was born that year and would go on to become the greatest magician in the world. Now in his nineties, he lives in his home north of London, and even his neighbors don't know that he used to be a superstar. But in the world of magicians, he is as revered as the Beatles are in the world of music. Magicians can be a fractious, argumentative group, and getting them to agree on anything is a challenge, but ask anyone who knows about the real work behind the magician's craft and they will all agree on David Berglas— even today, he is the best.

His life reads like a James Bond story. As the Gestapo knocked on their front door in Berlin, the teenage David Berglas and his family escaped down the back staircase and fled to London. There, he lied about his age and altered his passport in the army recruiting office so he could join the Allies and return to his homeland to fight the Nazis. After the war he could have done anything—he has a photographic memory and speaks three languages fluently—but chose to pursue a career as a professional magician. Quickly, his performances on the nascent BBC made David Berglas a household name in the United Kingdom.

A list of his illusions reads more like a litany of biblical miracles than performances by a magician. He once stopped the traffic in Piccadilly Circus. All of it. A black-and-white film clip of the moment shows the whole thing, but it was even more astonishing for the hundreds of pedestrians there that evening who saw it in person—one minute the cars are rushing through the intersection of Regent Street and Shaftesbury, and then Berglas raises his hands and everything just stops. The cars sit in the road. A dog stands still, front leg raised in midstride. A cyclist balances on two wheels, motionless. For a moment no one moves. Then Berglas claps his hands and the world resumes its business.

At a banquet in London, he made a grand piano vanish from the middle of the room while it was surrounded by party guests, leaving the piano player sprawled on the floor in shock. On a flight from London to New York, he pushed a playing card through the window of the airplane. It stuck there for a moment on the outside of the glass, just long enough for the reporter sitting next to him to identify it as the card on which he'd written his name, and then it caught the rushing air and peeled off into the sky.

Berglas approached his work as an outsider, independent of the traditional ploys and stratagems magicians have developed over the past few hundred years to amaze their audiences. He invented original magic with his own secret methods, and even the best magicians in the world couldn't explain it. Magicians flew to London from all over the world to watch Berglas work and returned home with accounts of his magic that sounded too incredible to believe.

Recently I met the great man at his home in London. "Nate," he said, before opening the door to his dining room, where we would spend the next five hours talking about magic, "you're married, aren't you?"

"I am."

"What is your wife's name?"

"Katharine."

"Very good," he said. "And of course you would know if she has a favorite flower."

"She does. Peonies."

Something happened then, and I'm not sure exactly what. Something shifted. He looked me directly in the eye, and even before he opened the door I understood why he was the greatest magician in the world. He had moved slowly as we walked down the hall, but now he was doing magic. He stood straight, filled with energy, and his words carried a weight that I have never been able to replicate.

"Let's sit in here," he said as he opened the door to the dining room. Inside I saw a large mahogany table with a vase at the center. The vase was filled with peonies.

"I love this room because it offers such a nice view of the garden," he said as he crossed the room and pulled aside the curtains, revealing a garden filled with peonies, two rows of lush green bushes covered with white blooms. I felt my knees go weak and I sat down quickly in one of the chairs. I have seen great magic performed by great magicians all over the world, but I had never felt like this before. This magic felt—real.

He sat down across from me and folded his hands in front of him. "I hope you'll tell Katharine about the flowers, and give her my regards."

I didn't understand the full extent of this magic until that night, when I spoke with Katharine by phone. I had left the Berglas residence late but had holed up in a pub to write down every scrap of detail about my time with the great magician. I didn't want to forget, and I didn't want to go to bed. Two Red Bulls, a beer, and nine or ten pages of manic scrawling later, I made my way back to where I was staying and called Katharine. She had gone to bed early, and even with the time difference she was already asleep, but when I told her about the peonies she sounded wide awake.

"You're sure they were peonies?"

"Yes. I'm sure. I know what peonies look like."

"Nate, that's impossible."

"Katharine, I was there. I saw them. I even touched the petals of the flowers on the table."

"And you saw them in the garden as well?"

"Yes. I'm positive."

For a moment she didn't say anything. Then she spoke.

"Nate, this is October. Peonies only bloom in May."

AFTER HOUDINI AND Berglas came a new breed of magicians who were recasting their art in the modern age. As I learned about magic as a teenager I discovered that the world I was trying so hard to enter was in the middle of a revolution. Around this time I heard the—apparently true—legend of Paul Harris, a magician who had lost everything in a house fire. Instead of rebuilding his home, he took to the road to answer one question: How do people respond to magic when they don't know they're watching a magician? He hitchhiked across the country doing magic for people in everyday situations and discovered how quickly a modern audience makes the jump from "magic trick" to "miracle" when they don't know they're at a magic show. His work was wild and unpredictable—not at all like the "showman" magic I had seen as a kid: no stage, no show, no performance. He'd just create impossible events and then walk away. Paul Harris was the Banksy of the magic world—a reclusive, enigmatic figure who emerged every once in a while with a masterpiece and then disappeared again into obscurity. His work was far more like a mural furtively spray-painted on a factory wall at night or a poem carved into the door of a bathroom stall with a pocketknife than a formal theatrical performance. The stories about his work were unlike anything I had ever heard. One day at a gas station he paid for a bottle of water and then changed the signature of the U.S. Treasurer printed on the dollar into the actual signature of the gas station attendant. No buildup, no presentation, just a moment of impossibility created for a complete stranger, and then he moved on.

When I was in high school, Paul Harris published a three-volume collection of his material for the magic community. I spent everything I had saved to buy a set, and when it arrived in the mail I stayed up all night to read it from front to back, all three volumes. He spoke of magic tricks as tools—"tools to unleash the moment," as he put it. The art wasn't in doing the trick, or even in making the trick, and it certainly wasn't in deceiving the audience. The art was in using magic to create a moment of astonishment and then getting out of the way.

Paul Harris's most famous student was David Blaine, whose *Street Magic* TV special changed everything for me when I saw it as a teenager. Blaine stripped away the flash and the spectacle from TV magic and made it accessible to everyone. He didn't need glitz to make people pay attention; he could build tension until it was almost unbearable with nothing but the force of his personality. A lesser magician would ease the moment with a joke, but Blaine just stood there waiting, like a gunslinger, and then he'd do the magic, break the tension, and everyone would just explode. With one hour of television Blaine showed that you don't need million-dollar budgets and full theatrical lighting rigs to do world-class magic on TV. All you needed was a deck of cards and an imagination.

THESE WERE MY heroes, and in the beginning I tried to be just like them. The gulf between wanting to become a great magician and actually doing it is enormous, however, and the career of a young magician is marked as much by a growing list of humiliations and public failures as it is by the occasional success. In high school I staged a show in the auditorium and my entire world came out to watch—six hundred friends, family members, girls from school, everyone I wanted to defy or impress. They all looked on in horror, fascination, and pity when my attempt at Blackstone's Floating Lightbulb illusion failed to float and in a panic I broke into an improvised dance to make it seem that nothing had gone wrong. I twirled about the stage, frantically trying to remember every bit of choreography from every David Copperfield special I had ever seen, and the audience sat mute, aghast, enduring the spectacle and waiting for the catastrophe to end.

A few years later in college I staged a Houdini-style underwater escape in the river that flowed through campus. I stood on a boat in the middle of the river wearing nothing but biking shorts and a thick snarl of chain, padlocks, and weights around my wrists and ankles. The sky was dead and gray and the water was dead and gray and a frigid breeze blew across its surface. I had delayed this stunt by two weeks because the river was still frozen. Now the ice had cleared and spring had come, reluctantly, but the water was still only 52 degrees at the surface, and colder in the depths below.

Technically, I succeeded. I jumped into the water, sank to the bottom, and escaped from the locks and the chains before swimming to the surface. But it didn't feel like a success. When Houdini did it he had ten thousand people turn up to watch. I had about a dozen who had stopped on their way to class, and after I got out the police showed up because someone had thought it was a suicide attempt.

I am living proof, though, that if you throw enough time and effort at something—maybe even anything—you can become good at it. Houdini once said, "The real secret to my success is simple: I work from seven in the morning to midnight and I like it." This quote lived on a scrap of paper stuck to the wall by my bed for ten years. I had hit Malcolm Gladwell's ten thousand hours of dedicated practice by the time I turned twenty-two, and he's right—I got pretty good.

★   ★   ★

IN THE FALL of my senior year of college, my friend Megan and I drove back to school after a short break and she asked me about my plans for after graduation. Megan and I knew each other in high school. She went to college to pursue her dream of becoming a writer—she published poetry under a pseudonym in a local literary magazine—and I went to pursue mine of becoming a magician, so when it came to the likelihood of finding gainful employment after graduation, we were perhaps two of the least promising students in the entire university.

"What are you going do when you're done?" she asked.

"What do you mean?"

"I mean, what are you going to do after graduation?"

"I'm going to be a magician."

She looked at me and I couldn't read her expression. Compassion, maybe, or sympathy.

"I know, Nate," she said, softly, "but what are you really going to do?"

"I think I'm going to Los Angeles."

"To do what? Just start doing magic for people?"

I had no idea. I hadn't thought that far ahead. Just north of here they filmed the movie *Field of Dreams*, and the film's tagline—*If you build it, they will come*—had epitomized my approach to working as an artist. If I became good enough, I reasoned, at some point someone would offer me a good salary to make my art.

"I guess, Megan. I'm sure it will work out."

"Nate," she said. "I don't think it works like that."

We sat in silence for a while.

I had been hearing this a lot, from everyone. I wanted to become the greatest magician in the history of the world.

Making this declaration as a nine-year-old is adorable. Making it as an adult is not, and I didn't have a backup plan. There was nothing else I wanted to do.

Highway 6 stretches and rolls across the most beautiful parts of Iowa—hills and fields, grazing sheep, weathered barns on well-worn lots—and in October the corn is high and ready for harvest. There's dust in the air from the farmers who have already taken in their crop, and when the sun is low in the sky the shafts of light shine down on everything and the whole world swells, expands, rises to the occasion. I think the animals could sense it, too. We watched a horse race across his field— playfully, joyfully at first, and then more purposefully—laying on speed, building up momentum, as though he wanted to leap over the fence and just keep going.

HOW TO BE A STARVING ARTIST

THE WEEK AFTER I finished school I drove from Iowa to Los Angeles to begin my career as a professional magician. I lived in a dorm for Japanese students studying English. My rent was cheap and it bought a closet-sized room with a desk, a chair, and a mattress on the floor with a sheet and pillow. These I shared with the cockroaches. My window was barred with vandal-proof grating, and everything looked broken and ugly, but above the neighboring buildings I had a good view of the sky and the perfect California sun, which is nice everywhere.

My room was down the hall from the bathroom and directly across from the shared kitchen. I became good at squeezing as much flavor as possible from cheap ingredients. Somewhere I got a box of fast-food mustard and pickle relish packets, and if you mix one of each into a can of tuna you get a kind of tuna salad you can eat with a fork. My staple was my own invention I called Magic Gruel and made in large batches: one can of black beans, one bag of cooked rice, and one jar of salsa all mixed together in a bowl and warmed in the microwave. I bought the ingredients in bulk and worked my way through them the whole summer.

My living arrangements were not the problem. My show
was the problem. No one came. Every Thursday night I did a
show at a rented theater in North Hollywood. This was my
only form of employment, and it didn't pay well. My marketing
budget was limited to a thousand postcards and one corner
ad in *LA Weekly* announcing the show. I spent one afternoon
sticking postcards on coffee shop bulletin boards and handing
them to anyone who made eye contact and hoped this would
be enough to pull in an audience. It wasn't. The theater held a
hundred seats but I never filled more than forty of them, and
after the cost of the rental I was just barely scraping a profit. This
wasn't nearly enough to cover rent or food, so I was paying a lot
to be a starving artist. Still, I was in Hollywood.

I probably should have gotten a side job but worried that I
had only this one shot to make it as a professional magician
and wanted to put every waking moment to good use. I spent
most of the time inventing new magic and reading. I found a
Blockbuster Video store a few miles away and rented a DVD set
of the greatest speeches of all time. A good magician works
with ideas more than props or tricks, and to communicate ideas
you need to know how to use words. I watched Churchill,
MLK, JFK, RFK, and Reagan, over and over, memorizing
their speeches. After working on magic all day, I'd climb into my
ailing Honda Civic and take the 101 through North Hollywood
to the 405 and blast down through Beverly Hills with the
windows open, delivering those speeches to the city below
until I understood how they worked and why they succeeded.
Churchill was a master. He preferred short, powerful words
because they hit with more force than longer ones, and he fired
them out at his opponents like cannonballs. I loved the Churchill

speeches. RFK was the best, though. He used silence better than anyone else in the world, creating tension, releasing it, making the audience hang on every word. He would have been a world-class magician.

I also discovered a magic shop a mile or so from my apartment. They sold the cheap jokes and gags in the front of the shop but in the back they had a vast collection of magic books by some of the greatest magicians in history. Once I proved I wasn't just looking for a stunt to do at a party, the owner of the store warmed up and started recommending books. I bought them with a credit card and took them back to my room. I'd read them that night and then again the next day before going back to the shop to tell him what I thought. He had found a good customer but I believe he was also thrilled to find such a voracious student. I was spending money that I didn't have, but I learned a lot.

Katharine and I had started dating the year before, and she had come to LA for an internship at UCLA so we could be together. We'd lived in the same hall in college and met one week when we ran into each other on the street, in the library, in the dining hall, everywhere. She reminded me of a pioneer or a frontier woman from the Old West—confident, tough, capable, curious—like she didn't quite fit into the modern age and must have come from somewhere else. I thought she was the most mysterious person I had ever met.

UCLA put her up in campus housing in Westwood. Santa Monica Boulevard stretches across Los Angeles from east to west and we lived essentially on the same street, but separated by forty-five minutes of driving and maybe ten thousand dollars per square foot of property value. Compared to my neighborhood, Westwood felt like Disney World. Some days I drove to the UCLA campus to read the magic books I couldn't afford on one of the benches outside their art museum and wait for her to be done. On the weekends we drove to the beach or went hiking in the hills. One afternoon we were goofing around and a dog named Norton ran away from his owner and caught our Frisbee in midair. You can still see his teeth marks in the plastic.

So we had some good adventures, but I couldn't escape from the crushing worry about money, and I was running out. I had spent most of my savings on the theater rental—*If you build it, they will come*—but I was losing hundreds of dollars a week. This was supposed to be the big launch of my career as a professional magician. As an artist I was better than ever, but I was learning quickly that you can be a good artist and still fail. One Thursday night I walked onstage and started the show.

"Wait, I'm sorry," I heard from the audience. "Am I really the only person here?"

I squinted through the stage lights and saw a middle-aged man sitting in the front row. He wore a thick green sweater even though it was July in Los Angeles, and he held a paperback novel open on his lap. He was the only one there.

I couldn't believe it. I knew ticket sales had been slow, but I'd hoped a few people would walk in at the last minute.

"I guess so," I said.

He rolled his eyes. "You mean I am the only person stupid enough to pay fifteen dollars for a ticket and drive all the way to North fucking Hollywood to see your show?"

I didn't say anything.

"I'm sorry," he said, "I'm going to go. Can I get my money back?"

"Maybe I could show you some magic one-on-one," I began.

"No thanks. I'm going to go." He stood up. I opened my wallet and handed him a ten and a five. He didn't make eye contact. Then he left. I stood onstage with the props for the show loaded in my back pocket. Two unopened water bottles waited on a stool. The room was empty.

"Hey Nate." The sound guy came out of the booth in the back. "That's pretty rough, brother. Can I buy you a beer?"

I looked up.

"No—thanks, though. I have the theater until midnight and I think I'm going to just hang out here for a bit."

"You got it. Have a good night. See you next week."

I stood in the room and looked out over all the empty seats. I had spent the week before working on a new illusion. It was a sharp twist on a classic illusion, keeping the same underlying structure but changing the way it played out for the audience so it felt surreal rather than spectacular. I didn't want to do magic that would shock, surprise, or dazzle. I wanted it to creep up on you like an episode of the *Twilight Zone*. I wanted it to make the hair on the back of your neck stand on end, like waking one morning to discover a hidden staircase in your house or a secret door you never noticed before in the back of a closet. C. S. Lewis got it exactly right. You don't find magic through a spell or a handful of enchanted beans. You find it just beyond the mundane and the everyday—a door behind some coats in the wardrobe that somehow leads to Narnia. And I knew I had found a way to put all of that into a magic trick. The night before, I'd stayed up until three or four, writing and rewriting the script for the performance and running though the presentation. It was ready, and I knew it was great. And now there was no one here to see it.

I looked down at the floor and then started going through the new piece anyway. Magic doesn't work without an audience. It's not like music, where you can close your eyes, turn up the volume on your guitar, and pretend you're playing for a packed house. Magic is interactive theater. You can practice the individual pieces, but it only ever exists in its entirety in the minds of the audience, so you can't do it justice in an empty room. Still, I wanted to see how it felt to move through the paces on a real stage.

I stood on the stage in the empty theater, trying at least for a moral victory. All I could hear was the audience from my show at Ames High—despite my failure with the lightbulb illusion they had stood at the end of the show, cheering and shouting so loud I could still hear it five years later. Now every seat was empty and I was in trouble. Every week I lost more and more money, and if I ran out I would have to move on, go home, or get a real job. I had risked everything on this summer in Los Angeles, and if it didn't work—if I didn't end the summer with an agent, a TV show, or some kind of employment as a magician—I didn't know how I could keep going.

~

THE WESTWOOD VILLAGE THEATER stood on a corner down the street from Katharine's apartment and I went there sometimes to spend more of the money I didn't have and see a movie.

The room was a vast, cavernous temple to the cinema—more than a thousand seats stretching back into the darkness, the screen rising like an altar. I went there to take refuge in the theater's air conditioning, see the movies, and think about magic. I was worried.

I was worried that movies were simply better than magic tricks as a vehicle for amazement. In Houdini's day the world had never seen *Star Wars*. They hadn't seen the dinosaurs of *Jurassic Park*. When Blackstone's audience watched his lightbulb float through the theater they had never seen the liquid metal Terminator chase Arnold on his motorcycle. As a young boy I had become interested in magic when I read the *Lord of the Rings* trilogy and imagined myself casting spells on the playground. Now you could go to the theater and see it all for yourself—not just the dragon or the ring, but also the magic. And it looked spectacular. Movies had reached a point where they could show you anything the director could imagine, and I worried that the modern audience was so inured to marvels that seeing the extraordinary had become an everyday occurrence. Turn on your television at any time of day and within about fifteen seconds of flipping through the channels you will see something—an alien, a superhero, a ghost or a monster or a spaceship hurtling through the heavens—that would have been miraculous in the golden days of magic.

How do you compete with *Star Wars*? How do you take an audience of people who have been to other worlds and other times, who have stormed the beaches of Normandy and watched the *Titanic* sink into the ocean, and show them anything that could register as even remotely amazing?

Houdini had worried about the same thing, even in those early days of cinema. Magicians revere him as a hero but forget that he spent much of the last half of his career trying to get out of the magic business. He wanted to become a movie star. He formed a production company—the Houdini Picture Corporation—and starred in a number of his own films. He played Quentin Locke, the secret agent for the justice department who used his abilities as an escape artist to solve crimes, track down bad guys, and fight for justice. He played Haldane, a secret service agent who used much of the same skill set to do much the same thing. His movies featured grand stunts that would have been impossible to perform in a theater—jumping from wing to wing of two flying biplanes, rolling under the wheels of a moving truck, swimming through the rapids to rescue a woman just feet from the edge of Niagara Falls. They weren't camera tricks. He actually did them.

One afternoon I walked down Sunset Boulevard looking for Houdini's star on the Hollywood Walk of Fame. I had assumed his star was awarded for his work as a magician—the first magician to earn such a star, I thought—but it wasn't. It was for his movies.

I saw a lot of movies that summer, and I learned something about the role of the magician. A filmmaker isn't using special effects to deceive an audience—they're not the purpose of the film but rather one of many little tools available to help bring the audience into another world in order to tell them something about this one. This is the key. A film can show you the most extraordinary, impossible occurrences and make them look absolutely real, but unless these impossibilities are used in the service of a story that can tell us something about ourselves and the plight of the human being in our own world, it's a bad movie. Ultimately a movie has to give you something real.

All of this may sound blindingly obvious to others, but for me it was a stark indictment of my own craft. With a few notable exceptions, the standard magic show had become pure entertainment, a progression of tricks, one after another, like a movie filled with car chases, explosions, and fight scenes but lacking characters, story, or soul. And because this is what the audience seemed to expect from a magic show—flashes of spectacle punctuated by snappy one-liners—how could you give them something else without losing them? How could you give them Stanley Kubrick when they expected—and *wanted*—Michael Bay?

I am not the first magician to identify this problem. That summer I came to see the theatrics of David Copperfield, the stark realism of David Blaine, and the artful construction of Penn and Teller's show as heroic attempts to pull away from the vapid, empty showmanship of the stereotypical magician and to give the audience an experience that rose above mere deception. I loved them for it. Some of these efforts worked better than others, and I had my own thoughts about how it should be done, but the discovery of this idea, or ideal—the magic trick as a vessel rather than an end in itself—changed the shape of my summer. I was broke and headed for imminent ruin, certainly, and no one was coming to my shows, but I felt as if I had discovered how to split the atom.

~

THE NEXT WEEK, attendance was better—I had maybe twenty people in to see the show. It went well, and afterward a man in his midthirties waited in the lobby to talk for a minute. He had a shaved head and wore black-rimmed glasses.

"You're probably losing a lot of money on this, aren't you?" he asked.

"Yeah."

"Well, you're an idiot. Did you rent this theater?"

"Yes."

"And did you do anything other than put an ad in *LA Weekly*?"

"Well, I handed out some postcards—"

"Yeah, you're an idiot. But that was a great show. It wasn't a very good show, mind you. Your transitions are terrible and I think you should probably get a haircut, but I like the intensity."

"Thank you," I said. His analysis of the show was right on— it wasn't very good in a technical sense, but I thought it contained a kernel of greatness and was thrilled that he had seen it, too.

"How old are you?" he asked.

"Twenty-two."

"Can I give you a piece of advice?"

"God, yes."

"You don't want to be here. Come back to LA when you have a name and a marketing budget. Go out and do a thousand shows somewhere else. Learn how to play to your strengths. Learn to cover your weaknesses. Right now you're just flailing around up there."

I felt deflated and didn't know what to say.

He pointed to the untouched stack of postcards on the table in the lobby advertising the *Nate Staniforth Magician* show. "Can I take one of these?" I nodded. They certainly weren't doing much good there on the table. He studied it, and then turned it over and read the back.

"Good luck, Nate. I'll see what I can do."

A WEEK LATER, I got a call from an agent asking if I'd like to do a college tour. Just like that. I couldn't believe it. I was at Katharine's apartment when the call came in. She could tell the call was important, and we stood in her kitchen with our heads together and the phone between us so we could both listen. Afterward we danced around the room as if we had survived a shipwreck and finally made it to shore.

TOUR

A MAGICIAN'S TOUR IS like a fisherman's voyage. For months the fishermen live on land, laying in stores and preparing their ship. Then one day they disappear to the sea and enter another world where the bureaucracy of daily life falls away. At sea, life shrinks to the immediacy of the job at hand and the relentless pursuit of the fish drives the passage from day into night and night into day far more than any turning of the globe. When Melville wrote of the voyage in *Moby-Dick* he knew that intent and purpose guide such an expedition far more than landmarks, charts, or celestial navigation. The actual location never matters. A magician's tour, like a true sea voyage, is a place unto itself, a wilderness somehow larger than the sum of cities, venues, hotels, and airports within it. It's a place of constant, restless, searching movement—a hunting ground where you leave behind home and table and bed and go out to find what you are looking for. "It's not down on any map," Melville wrote. "True places never are."

When I began touring I was unprepared for every aspect of the journey. The scope, the scale, the late nights, the early mornings. Any sense of accomplishment at finally being able to tour with my show was replaced within the first week or so by the realization that I had ventured into the deep and didn't know how to swim.

~

WHEN YOU'RE SUCCESSFUL you can plan your tour so you work your way slowly across the country, doing a show in one town and then performing in the next town a few hundred miles away the next night. But when you're just starting out you go wherever you can get work, and so a tour schedule ends up hauling you from one side of the country to another from day to day, and you might cross the country four times in a week just to work as often as possible. No one pays you for the nights you're not working, so during a tour you try to do a show every night if you can.

The days often began in the middle of the night. On most mornings the alarm rang at three o'clock, maybe three thirty, and I'd get up to take a shower. If I had remembered to preload the hotel room coffee machine I'd flip the switch before heading into the bathroom, but hotel coffee was always a mixed blessing: it wasn't so much the bad taste but the fact that with two roller suitcases I didn't have any extra hands to hold a cup on my way to the car, and I certainly wasn't going to sit in the hotel room at three in the morning to casually sip a cup of coffee. The ability to maximize sleep by relentlessly paring down the time needed to get ready in the morning comes early in the life of a frequent traveler. If the flights were delayed or traffic clogged the roads and made the drive longer than expected, I might have to walk onstage in whatever I was wearing, so this required at least a minimal amount of care. Still, I could go from a dead sleep to walking out the door in twelve minutes, including a shower.

At this hour the day looked bleak. Ahead, I'd have a two-hour drive to the airport in Charlotte, for instance, followed by a three-hour flight to Minneapolis before my connecting flight to Seattle for the show that night. When I landed in Washington I'd have about an hour to get my bags, pick up the rental car, and check in to the hotel before I was due at the venue for load-in, sound check, and, finally—after fourteen hours of travel and preparations—the show, after which I would return to the hotel and get four hours of sleep before waking up and doing the same thing again the next day. And the next day. And the next day.

The trick was to ignore the long-term view of the day and break everything down into a series of next steps. Later I'd run through the show in my mind and prepare for the jarring act of walking out onto the stage in front of five hundred people, but at three o'clock in the morning, the show was still in the far-off, unthreatening future. As I climbed into the rental car and opened the can of coffee strategically purchased the night before and left to chill in the cold car overnight—a detail that looks pitiful and pathetic as I write it here but felt in this predawn hour like a monumental, day-changing victory—the tasks immediately ahead of me were simple. I'd drive for two hours through the dark, sleeping North Carolina countryside. I'd drink my can of coffee. I'd listen to Dan Carlin, probably, or maybe NPR. And in this way—step by step, day by day, I would tour my show around the country.

KATHARINE AND I had been married in the summer and lived in a small apartment in Chicago with a beautiful old cast-iron bathtub and unreliable hot water. I was twenty-three years old and Katharine was two years younger. She worked as a nurse and I gave almost a hundred performances that first season. Sometimes, on the rare occasions when we were together, Katharine and I would walk to the grocery store down the street and buy a cheap bottle of wine to share after dinner, and if I had a particularly good month we might go to the Thai restaurant a few blocks from our apartment and sit on the rooftop patio with noodles and beer. But mostly I was on the road, and when I was away I felt as if I had been gone forever.

One evening I finished a show in Virginia and flew to Spokane, Washington, first thing the next morning. The drive to Moscow, Idaho, from Spokane follows the state highway along the creek through Hangman's Valley and then climbs abruptly through the hills to a long, high plain of grassland running on and gently upward. If your timing is good you'll have the road to yourself. You'll rise and fall with the road and follow it between hills as it stretches away to the south, and if you didn't love this part of the country when you started, you will by now. It looks like Scotland, or the wilder parts of Iowa, but much closer to the sky.

All of this would have been easier to appreciate if I hadn't felt like death. I had a terrible case of the flu and a plastic bag from the gas station ready in the front seat in case I couldn't pull over in time. When I got to the Super 8 motel in Moscow I spent an hour propped up against the toilet. Then I took a shower, changed my clothes, and drove to the theater.

By the time I finished setting up the show backstage I knew I was in trouble. I looked pale and was having a hard time keeping water down, and I'm sure I was dehydrated. On the back of one of my tour posters I had written out a new set list for the show and taped it to the front of the stage. I had scrapped most of the audience participation because I didn't want to have anyone up there with me if I had to run offstage, but this meant I was going to have to talk more than usual, and I was worried about so much talking. When you're trying to communicate with an entire audience you use your whole body and fling your words to the back of the room with your eyes and your fingers and your intentions as much as your voice, and I didn't know how I'd be able to do that for an hour when I couldn't even keep a sip of water down for more than a few minutes.

Before the show I called Katharine to tell her how badly everything was going and she gave me the best pep talk she could, but you go into something like this on your own no matter what anyone else says to you beforehand.

The theater at the University of Idaho was in a Gothic stone cathedral of a building and I walked onstage just before night-fall. The setting sun glowed through the stained glass windows and you never get used to walking into a room and having five hundred people start shouting and applauding. It's overpowering. The difference between this moment and the one just before it stunned me to silence. For a moment I didn't know what to say.

When I launched into the opening speech I could feel the strength coming back and the illness draining away and for the moment I had everything I needed. I abandoned the new set list and threw myself into the performance with everything I had, and I couldn't believe the vast reservoir of energy at my disposal. I used all of it. The audience rose to the occasion and I felt I had reached a new level as a performer—as if whatever I had felt under the piano so many years before was close, hovering some-where ahead and just out of reach.

During intermission I threw up in the garbage can backstage. Then I went out and finished the show, and at the end the audience stood up in one motion and cheered for a long time. I felt like a runner at the end of a long race—ready to fall down, but grateful. I went back to the hotel with a fever and slept in my stage clothes on top of the bed without ever climbing under the covers.

~

ASIDE FROM THE very modest living I was scraping together from these shows, the true benefit of the tour was the time I got onstage in front of an audience. This is the real difference between professionals and amateurs. A number of extraordinarily gifted magicians support their love of magic with outside careers as lawyers or bank managers. For some people—and maybe most people—learning and performing magic is a way to scratch an itch that can't be scratched any other way. Inventing and building new illusions is a rigorous exercise in lateral thinking and problem solving, like chess, but sometimes you get to play with a soldering torch. Also, the amateur magician has a tremendous advantage over the professional. When you buy a ticket to a magic show, you know you are seeing a magician, and this context—*We're going to a theater to see a show*—fundamentally shapes the way you perceive the magic. An amateur can go under cover. An amateur can weave impossibilities into the fabric of daily life and create wondrous, unimaginably strange moments for friends, family, and co-workers who will not be able to dismiss them so easily as magic tricks performed by a professional.

But if you want to perform your magic in a theater, there's no substitute for putting in hours and hours onstage in front of an audience. You learn the difference between doing magic and performing it, and then you learn that the actual difference is between performing magic and communicating it. Magic is a social experience as much as a sensory one, and the only way to learn how to take an audience and lead them by the hand to a place where they actually believe in magic is to first go through all the wrong ways of doing it and learn from those mistakes. It's like Churchill said: "You can always count on the Americans to do the right thing, after they've tried everything else." This is how you learn to be a magician, by trying everything and finally doing it right.

So as I crossed the country doing shows in lecture halls, auditoriums, and student unions, I learned things about magic I had never imagined. I learned how to do a card trick so that even the people in the back row of an eight-hundred-seat theater could follow the action. I learned how to turn hecklers into allies and allies into anchors I could lean on during a performance if things got rocky. I learned when to be loud and when to be quiet, when to build momentum and when to slow down, and how to use comedy like a tactical strike to disarm, distract, or dominate as the situation required.

I learned other things, too. I discovered how elusive and unpredictable the experience of wonder could be. You really can't create it. Other responses, such as fear, shock, suspense, surprise, and laughter are created through the building and releasing of tension in an audience and can be reliably reproduced from night to night. On tour I'd record each show and play it back afterward to study the constant ebb and flow of tension running through a performance. With time you could learn from each show and make changes the next night: hold the pause here, speed up there, store up as much tension as possible in one moment so you can burn it all like rocket fuel in the next. Stand-up comedians do this, too.

But wonder was far less predictable. You could deceive, inspire, or entertain an audience all evening without ever coming anywhere near the sense of still, silent majesty I associate with the word "wonder." Sometimes it would show up and pass through the room like an electric current, and sometimes it wouldn't, like a flighty, unpredictable friend who stops by unannounced from time to time but can never be trusted to keep an appointment. I learned to structure a show to accommodate this unpredictability, giving the moment room to breathe if that sense of wonder took hold of an audience but always having a backup plan if it didn't make an appearance.

More than anything else, I learned that this goal of giving people the experience of wonder was as important as the tools you used to do it; that *intent* mattered as much as ability. An audience who sensed you were just there to deceive them would turn on you, but an audience who understood that you were there to share something valuable with them would hang on every word. You couldn't just do one trick after another. You had to build something. Build a castle. Build a cathedral. And then invite the audience inside.

THE EXHAUSTION OF being on the road was overpowering, and mostly there are strange moments I only half-remember, distinct but unconnected to anything around them, as if they were never anything more than a dream even as they happened. One night a man climbed up onto the arms of his chair in the theater, pointed at me onstage from across the room, and shouted, "To hell with you! You're the devil! I'm out of here!" Another night at a college in Florida, campus security barged into the dining hall in the middle of a show because they thought a riot had broken out.

I vaguely remember driving out to a glacier after a show one night in Juneau, Alaska, to look for bears with a group of college students before they dropped me at the airport for my midnight flight to the next show in the next city. Sitting at a Denny's eating pancakes and drinking coffee at two A.M. and writing Katharine an email on my laptop before getting back in the car and driving on to make the six A.M. flight from somewhere to somewhere else. Sleeping in my car at a campsite along the Pacific Coast Highway one night because I couldn't make it all the way to San Francisco. Walking New Orleans alone at night, past rows of fortunetellers with tarot cards and a woman behind a folding table who said she could read the lines on the palm of my hand and tell me the future. I can still feel the weight of the air and the warm wind blowing down the street like a courier from another world. But then it all disappears, or maybe it never happened.

Here's what I know. The combination of travel, performance, caffeine, and adrenaline muddled the days and nights of the tour schedule into one unrelenting blur. I'd arrive at the airport after hours of driving and then sleep while my body hurtled across the continent, curled up in my window coach seat with my hood up, sunglasses on, and earplugs in. I'd wake on the other side of the country with no spatial understanding of where I was or where I had been. Then I'd spend the day in the depths of a sunless theater preparing for the show. Then I'd do it again and again and again. I was never really in Georgia. I was never really in Tennessee. I was on Tour. And Tour was its own place—a secret nation of

airports, hotels, rental car counters, loading docks, and theaters—
where you'd leave a hotel at three in the morning, cross the
country, do a show, and then check in to an identical hotel at
midnight. Same design. Same lobby. Same carpet. Outside the
world rushed by the windows of the planes and the cars while I
hung on, incredulous, and tried not to fall off.

～

AT FIRST, IT all felt like an adventure. I couldn't believe I was
actually pulling this off. Before I started touring, I had never
been east of Chicago. Now, in the busiest times of year, I'd
connect through Chicago's O'Hare airport seven days a week.
Every morning I'd get my coffee at the Starbucks by the C
concourse and one morning the barista asked if I worked in one
of the terminals. "No," I replied. "I just fly through every day."

I felt like I had been everywhere—Savannah, Georgia;
Lancaster, Pennsylvania; Havre, Montana. One day I was in
Pocatello, Idaho—a town nestled in a valley ringed by high
hills and mountains capped with snow. The air was cool and
crisp and the sky was deep blue and I thought I had never been
anywhere as beautiful as Pocatello.

"This place is incredible," I said to the promoter of the show
when we met outside the theater.

She looked at me curiously. "Pocatello? Really?"

"Yeah," I said. "We don't have mountains in Iowa. This is
amazing."

"I don't know," she replied. "You just kind of get used to it."

FAKE

O N T O U R I discovered the thrill of a standing ovation, but I also learned the sharp sting of an indifferent audience and the lingering humiliation of a bad show. Often this was my fault. Maybe I didn't connect with the audience, maybe an illusion fell flat. Sometimes I could blame the venue—one night at a college somewhere on the East Coast the student activities board arranged to have twenty or thirty pizzas delivered during the middle of the show for everyone in the audience. You can imagine how that disrupted the performance. But frequently I felt the resistance of something else, larger and more stubborn, like an invisible wall, and I didn't know how to get around it.

I had learned by this point that some people do not like magic. For many, the word brings to mind laser beams, smoke machines, and tight leather pants. It conjures images of Las Vegas showmen, of style without substance, of overblown, underwhelming spectacle heavy on cliché and light on actual ideas. In the 1920s, Houdini was a mainstream star and magic was in its golden age. Now magic is largely seen as something for children. It's ignored by adults, or derided, or tolerated for brief periods of time now and then—for really, everyone loves to be amazed—but only rarely, and ideally with a thick protective layer of irony wrapped around the experience.

Good magic isn't cool. It can't be cool. Cool is divisive. Cool is exclusionary. Cool does not sit next to the new kid at lunch, and good magic is all about sitting next to the new kid at lunch. So I expected a certain amount of indifference. But as I traveled the country with my show I came to understand the great divide between my understanding of what a magician could be and the popular perception held by the general public. For most people, magic was cheap. Magic was low. At its best, magic offered a brief moment of light diversion. At its worst—and in the eyes of many it was frequently at its worst—magic was a vapid, frustrating, even pathetic waste of time.

One night during a college tour I was scheduled to appear as the opening act for a poetry reading. I was thrilled. I thought a group of people who had gathered to hear poetry might be more open to the experience of magic than an audience who wanted nothing more than a good time. Wonder is a delicate, fragile state, and while I had become good at using my craft like a wrecking ball to knock a hole in the perception of a belligerent audience so they could look through and see it for a moment, I was excited to discover what I could do with an audience who had shown up already looking for a meaningful encounter with an artist's work.

When I got to the venue I could tell something was wrong. The organizer of the event stood onstage talking to a man in his midfifties—the poet, I would later learn—who peered at me when I walked in the room and then returned to the argument. I caught the words "magician" and "ridiculous" before he raised his voice.

"I just don't think it's appropriate," he barked.

Even now I think about the sting of that moment frequently. He had never seen me work, but to him it didn't matter. Magic was just magic, after all. Certainly it wasn't poetry.

Modern society's antipathy toward magic is perfectly embodied in the fictional character of Gob Bluth—a mocking, derisive caricature of a magician from the hit TV series *Arrested Development*—and the American public embraced him with glee. Gob personified the stereotypical magician completely: the clueless bombast, the bravado, the self-absorbed overconfidence unsupported by any actual talent, and—this more than anything else—his conviction that magic was a serious art form deserving of respect and attention. In one scene from the show's first season a group of magicians held a protest rally and one raised a sign reading WE DEMAND TO BE TAKEN SERIOUSLY! The joke, of course, is that the idea of taking a magician seriously is laughable.

At first I took it personally. My show has none of the Las Vegas stereotypes. I don't tell jokes or use smoke machines, and I had seen enough audiences respond well to my work that I knew it was at least possible for an intelligent audience to lose themselves in amazement during my show. Night after night I'd watch individuals in the audience begin the show with their arms crossed, heads down, obviously skeptical, as if they had come for no other reason than to figure everything out. Over the next ninety minutes many of them would thaw out and respond with the same astonishment and wonder as the children in the next row, but then the show would end and they would close back up even before leaving their seats, as though they had bumped into an old friend while walking down the street but now had to hurry along on their way. Sometimes they spoke with me after the show. "I just want the answer," they'd say, forgetting that I had seen them during the performance, laughing, wondering, eyes wide. They didn't *just* want the answer. They wanted the mystery, too.

Here was an enigma, I thought, and one reaching far beyond the response to a magic show. Every night onstage I witnessed a tension in the human spirit between our longing to revel in a mystery and our impulse to destroy it. I came to see the modern resentment toward magic as a clue to some larger struggle in our culture, like a small ripple in a pond revealing the monster lurking just below the surface of the water.

One night in New Jersey a group of people gathered at the front of the stage after the show for pictures, and a woman in the group kept insisting I tell her how one of the illusions was done. I think she was a reporter for the college paper—nineteen, I'm guessing, and not even trying to be nice.

"Why are you doing this?" she finally asked.

"What do you mean?"

"It's all fake," she said. "I know it's fake. So you can tell me how you did it."

I wanted to explain that magic is fiction. Like a writer of fiction, a magician does everything possible to make an illusion feel real in the moment. Good books feel real. Good movies feel real. Good magic feels real, too. I wondered if she was upset with J. D. Salinger for inventing Holden Caulfield, as if any of the power of *Catcher in the Rye* depended on its being the story of an actual teenager.

But she was having none of it.

"So why can't you tell me? If it's not real, are you just keeping it a secret because it makes you feel powerful?"

"Do I look particularly powerful to you right now?" I asked. This was not going well.

"Whatever," she said. "I'm just going to Google it." And she walked away.

I'm just going to Google it. There. In one sentence she had identified something new in the world—some new way of seeing things, or of thinking about things. Here was the cynicism of our modern age, and I despised it. Information is now so easy to find that few of us are strong enough to resist the temptation of presuming we already know more than we actually do. Our worldviews are still built on the foundations of our own limited understanding, but we now live under the dangerous illusion that they are reinforced and supported by all of the knowledge that has ever existed. *If I don't have the answers now, I can find them,* the thinking goes, and without even noticing we shrink our world down to the size of our certainties.

Here is a blind spot in our culture, created both by the habitual, almost systemic mistaking of information for understanding and by the assumption that a complete understanding of anything can be attained with enough information. This view of the world reduces everything and everyone to bits of data—some known, some still unknown, but all knowable—and reduces wonder to a mere absence of information, as if the simple brute fact of our own existence isn't mystery enough to keep you up for a week if you really consider it. *"Oh that,"* we so easily say about anything we don't understand, *"I'm sure we have that all sorted out."* And in doing so we insulate ourselves from any facts, opinions, and ideas—those pesky things—that ask us to venture away from our own view of reality.

I suppose we have the right to remain ignorant, but we are in the world. And in the world, our actions have an impact on others, so assuming that you understand something you don't becomes an ethical issue more than an intellectual one. There is a danger and maybe even a violence to the belief that you already know something—or someone—completely, when you do not, and will not, and cannot. Knowledge does not allow you to understand the world. Knowledge dispels the illusion that you understand the world.

To be sure, I don't have magical powers, and the college reporter was right that my show was, in one sense, totally fake. So are the dinosaurs in *Jurassic Park*. So are the pirates in *Peter Pan*. Tinker Bell isn't real either. But the universe is not made only from facts—take, for instance, kindness, loyalty, love, or wonder—and treating information as the only thing that matters makes it impossible to see the rest.

~

As I traveled across the country doing my show, I wanted to understand how my craft had become synonymous with Las Vegas glitz when every night onstage I could see the obvious potential for it to be more.

Magic is ancient. Every culture in the world has its own version of the Magician, an archetypal figure who has been around as long as anyone can remember. The Westcar Papyrus in the Berlin Museum describes the story of an Egyptian named Dedi who lived around 4000 B.C. and was renowned for his feats of magic. The Pharaoh summoned Dedi and ordered him to demonstrate his powers, so Dedi took one of the Pharaoh's geese and pulled off its head. He put the head on one side of the room, the body on the other, and then stood between them to cast an incantation and say his magic words. The headless goose stood up. It began hopping across the room toward its severed head, and when it arrived the two were rejoined by magic and the goose began to honk. Magicians still perform this feat today.

But long before the magicians of ancient Egypt came the shamans, the witch doctors, and the medicine men of tribal cultures. Their names vary from place to place and each carries its own nuance, but broadly speaking, their roles are some combination of healer, prophet, magician, and priest. Some use sleight of hand and ceremony in their work—an engraving dated to 1896 shows the shaman of the Menomini Native American tribe producing and vanishing snakes from a cloth bag, for instance, and I was fascinated that someone could use magic tricks for such a wildly different purpose than how they're commonly used today.

But I wasn't interested in the anthropology of tribal magic for its own sake. I was trying to solve a problem. I wanted to understand how a shaman could perform the same type of magic—snakes vanishing in a bag, as I mentioned—and do it in such a way that the audience and the community embraced the experience instead of dismissing it or explaining it away. I had discovered the discrepancy between the strong response I'd get from the audience during a show and the indifference most people have for magic everywhere else, and I thought that someone who understood both magic in the modern world and the shaman's work in the tribal world would at least be able to see the problem in its entirety.

David Abram is an ecologist, author, activist, and—this last point is a source of boundless pride for me—a magician. His book *Spell of the Sensuous* blew a lot of minds in the magic community, mine included. In it he discusses the role of the magician in tribal and traditional cultures, opening with the story of his adventure into the rain forests of Bali and the mountains of Nepal where he pretended to be an actual, supernaturally gifted magician to see if he could study the work of the indigenous shaman from the inside. His book was a constant companion with me on tour, and if you wanted to identify the source of my conviction that climbing on top of a table in a bar in Chicago and challenging the entire audience to a fight was acceptable behavior for a working, professional magician, Abram's book—with his vision of magic as a natural, wild, irrepressible force within the human experience—would be it. There, far more than in the caricatures of magic so ubiquitous in pop culture, I saw a reflection of my own experience as a magician.

Abram argues that the tribal magician's main role was as an ambassador between the tribe and its environment, an intermediary between the immediate and the infinite who used the craft of magic not as an end to itself but as a way of ensuring the tribe's good standing in the world around it. The tribal magician worked as an emissary to ensure friendly relations between the tribe and the sky, the rain, the forest, the world. For a magician whose early interest in magic came from the night sky, this was a revelation. Magic was a tool, to be used not for the pleasure of the audience or the ego of the magician but as a way to maintain balance and equilibrium between the local community and the rest of the universe.

In the shaman's work, "magic" was a tangible, practical force as necessary to the daily life of the tribe as hunting or agriculture. The shaman worked to ensure a good crop, or a good rain, or a good catch of fish when the tribe went out to sea. When the anthropologist Bronislaw Malinowski studied the way the Melanesian people of New Guinea use ceremonial magic to aid them in their fishing, he noticed that they never used it when fishing close to shore or in the safety of a lagoon where they were shielded from the danger and uncertainty of the open sea. There they didn't need it, or it didn't work. Their magic helped them only when they ventured out farther into the danger of the open ocean, past the point where their skill could ensure a safe and successful voyage, and there they relied on it extensively. The shaman was there to intercede on their behalf, asking the ocean for safe passage and a successful haul of fish and ensuring that the tribe and the ocean remained on good terms.

The contrast between this tribal shaman and the modern magician of today was obvious. The tribal communities had a different understanding of the relationship between "magic" and "reality" and had not drawn a line between them. The work of the shaman was not all that different from, say, the work of the fisherman. Both were a part of the daily process of living and each was connected to the other. But the Western magician operates in a culture where magic has no place in the daily movements of society, so it exists in the face of civilization rather than as a natural expression of it.

"Most magicians end up performing somewhere like Las Vegas," Abram elaborated in an interview after he published his book. "They see themselves as 'illusionists'—as people trying to create the illusion of magic. But they themselves don't believe in magic. What a sad state the craft of magic has fallen into in the world. It would be as if most musicians and concert artists didn't really believe that real music existed. Then you would have pianists who had pianos with flashing lights all over them and women dancing in sequins around them as they played their flashy music. Magic has been reduced to that in the West. It really doesn't exist for us anymore."

A few weeks after the performance in New Jersey, I was in the middle of a show in Pennsylvania and I could tell that the audience had gotten away from me. I lost them a few minutes into the performance, and even after a prolonged struggle to regain their good faith, I began the last act of the show knowing I still didn't have it. On this particular leg of the tour I was closing the show with an escape from a straitjacket, and when I asked for volunteers to restrain me, eager hands shot up throughout the theater. Two massive young men vaulted up to the stage and they spent the next five minutes binding me so tightly that I couldn't stand upright. I was at their mercy. As they wrapped the straps around my body, the jeers rose from the audience, one after another.

"You've got him!"

"Get him!"

"Make it hurt!"

This last one got my attention. I caught the heckler's eye— front row, just a few years younger than me. He had his fist up in the air. He looked right at me as he shouted again.

"Get him!" he called. "Make it hurt!"

The show hadn't been great, but this was too much. I had been amazed before at the way a simple magic trick could create so much wonder and joy. At this show, I witnessed the other side. These people had seen what I had to offer and some of them had genuinely hated it.

The music began.

I'd been using part of the rondo from Beethoven's Sonatina Number 2 in F—a thin, eerie melody—to contrast with the brutality of the escape from the straitjacket. The secret to the straitjacket escape is simple. You just do it. There is no secret method other than the agonizing, inch-by-inch struggle to slowly extricate one hand and then another before unbuckling the rest of the straps. As I writhed on the floor, fighting for each inch of slack necessary to free my first hand, the audience drowned out the music. Maybe half of them were with me, but half were very much against me.

Where had this anger come from?

Afterward—after the eventual escape, the ending of the show, the drive back to the hotel—I thought about the enmity my show had created in that audience. It wasn't new. I had seen it before, expressed differently but still there. But that night it had reached a fever pitch, and I saw something there I hadn't seen before.

The antipathy and resentment felt toward magicians is not just because magicians are ridiculous. Sometimes we are, but our society is filled with ridiculous people doing ridiculous things. It doesn't come just from the hype, the bombast, the over-the-top showmanship so often associated with the magician's craft. Hype and bombast are all around us. Look at the music industry. Or reality TV.

The anger—and I do believe it is anger—toward the modern magician comes from the way even a simple magic trick done well can reach uninvited into the deepest hopes of a person. Sometimes this can be an uncomfortable reminder. People have hard lives, and something like magic that promises a moment of real joy or even a new way of seeing the world threatens to unseat whatever insulation they have managed to erect between themselves and that hardness, whether it's cynicism, nihilism, escapism, or elitism. The cultural resentment toward magic comes from the sadness found in the space between the universal human longing to believe in magic and the overwhelming evidence all around us that there is no such thing. It's not that a modern audience doesn't want magic. It's that they want it so badly but have already decided it's not out there, and dislike being told that maybe they were looking in the wrong place.

HOW TO LIGHT YOURSELF
ON FIRE

A S A TOURING magician I lived a strange dual life, and I'm not sure my neighbors knew quite what to think of me. Katharine and I had moved to a quiet neighborhood in Iowa near the edge of town, and for six months of the year I operated like a relatively normal freelancer working from home. I spent my days designing magic in my studio in the basement, but I could have been editing wedding photos, creating websites, or doing whatever it is that self-employed people do when they work from home. In the evenings I walked the dog with Katharine, and on Sundays we had a bonfire and a standing invitation to friends and family to come by for dinner. I ran. I mowed the lawn. I went to the grocery store.

But then I would disappear, and for months the only clues to my existence were the cabs idling in my driveway at four in the morning to take me away or, occasionally, the ones that brought me back from the airport days or weeks later. I would emerge, haggard and pale, wearing dark sunglasses and a motorcycle jacket instead of my usual blue jeans and T-shirt, and haul two enormous suitcases out of the trunk of the taxi and drag them to the front door of my house before going inside, closing the blinds, and sleeping like the dead.

Originally, coming home to see Katharine on my days off had seemed like a good idea, but the exhaustion of flying back to Iowa from the East Coast or the West Coast or wherever the last run of shows had ended just for a day or two at home before setting out again wore on both of us. One evening I arrived home at six o'clock for what amounted to a ten-hour leave from the tour. We ordered Thai food and went to bed early, and when Katharine woke in the morning I was already up and on an airplane headed out for the show that night.

"Goodbye, Katharine," I had whispered earlier that morning, already dressed, when the bedroom was still dark and the taxi waited with its lights off in the driveway.

She stirred. Her eyes half-opened, and she said, "We sure have a lot of goodbyes in our life, don't we."

"We do."

"More than most people."

"More than almost anyone."

"Except the president, probably," she said, stretching her arms above her head, arching her back, and then burying herself back into the sheets and falling asleep.

I turned and walked down the hallway. I closed the front door as quietly as I could and clipped my house key to its ring inside my bag, where I wouldn't see it again for another week.

Two hours later Katharine's alarm would wake her. She'd get up, make coffee, feed the dog. She'd get ready for work and take the bus to the hospital, where she'd enter a world completely unknown to me. Then she'd take the bus home again, make dinner, feed the dog again, and maybe see her friends in the evening. We'd talk by phone before the show or maybe after, and then she'd turn out all the lights in the house except the one by our bed so she could read until she was too tired to see the words on the page, and then hopefully she'd fall asleep and not think of me again until her alarm woke her the following morning.

Occasionally we'd be out together for dinner and someone would ask her what it's like to be married to a magician. This is what it's like.

∽

THAT NIGHT—HOMESICK, angry, and stricken with the fear that finds me about an hour before every show and stays with me until I go on—I walked onstage in Reno, Nevada, to find 750 people crammed into a gorgeous red velvet jewel box of a theater. The next ninety minutes were almost incandescent. By the second act the momentum had become a tangible, palpable force to be gathered carefully one moment and cracked like a whip the next. The audience was wild and exuberant. They leaned forward in their chairs, dead silent and watching everything, and then the magic happened and they shouted like the room was on fire. In this crucible of my efforts onstage everything else in my life burned away—the travel, the strain, the time away from home—and all that remained was one untainted moment of exhausted, exultant joy.

"Good night," I said, and the entire room was on its feet. But what I really meant was *Thank you*. All of a sudden I was in the cornfield on the edge of the world again, and there, for just a moment, I felt I could see forever.

∽

THE HOUR AND a half onstage each night was the only thing keeping me going, but even that wasn't enough, and I knew I was wearing thin. At first I don't think anyone else noticed, but by this point the strain was beginning to show. When I pulled in to the hotel later that night I sprang for valet parking—a minor luxury made large by the twenty-hour day preceding it—and on the way inside I passed a gaunt, haunted-looking man wearing an immaculate white suit and fedora. He leaned against a cane, like a displaced aristocrat, smoking a cigar and looking very much like the devil, or Kevin Bacon. He tipped his hat as I approached the door. "Cheerio, Desperado."

What the hell? Did he just call me Desperado?

I didn't say anything. I was tired and ready for bed. I disappeared into the hotel, checked in at the front desk, and found the elevator, already half-asleep and running the math for the next few hours as the doors closed—ten minutes to get ready for bed, four hours until the alarm, twelve minutes to shower and dress, fifteen minutes to—

A black cane with a golden cobra head for a handle snaked between the elevator doors just before they closed. The doors opened. There stood the devil/Kevin Bacon.

"I was just heading up myself," he said. He spoke with a vaguely Southern drawl, as if he had traveled to Reno from South Carolina, or Hell.

I stared at him, speechless. He was sixty, maybe sixty-five, with bright blue eyes and a thin white mustache carefully trimmed to turn up at the edges. He looked like a wolf, smiling and hungry. The elevator doors closed behind him. We were alone.

He leaned against the wall of the elevator and held up one finger, as if silencing an entire room. Then he delicately pressed the button for the top floor and turned his attention to me.

"Reno is a strange town," he said.

"Yes," he continued, "Reno is a *very* strange town. But can I tell you something *in confidence?* We are not in Reno. Do you know where we are?" He leaned closer. "We are in the Twilight Zone."

For some reason I agreed. He smiled and leaned back.

"What do you do for a living?"

"I'm a magician," I said. Usually this elicits surprise or, at the very least, incomprehension—*Did you say musician? What instrument do you play?* But the devil/Kevin Bacon didn't react at all. He looked at me, studying, uncertain of something. It was the only time in my life I have actually believed in mind reading. It felt as if he looked all the way through me and saw something everyone else had missed.

The bell rang and the elevator door opened to my floor. He held up a finger, unmoving, unblinking, blocking my way and peering at me, still searching.

"No," he said finally, just before stepping aside. "You are not a magician. You are a desperado."

Desperado. It stayed with me for the rest of the night. *Desperado,* from the Spanish *desesperado.* "One without hope."

～

IN A WAY, I had seen this disillusionment coming for years. Every child has the experience of looking up at the adults of the world and wondering *What happened to you? You were my age once. What did you lose between there and here?* And as a young boy learning magic I saw this loss everywhere. The napkin levi-tated, the playing card changed color, the coin vanished, and suddenly the contrast between how people usually act and their astonishment in those moments was impossible to ignore.

I came to see this loss—or whatever it is that causes this loss—as an enemy to be fought and repelled at all costs. One night as a child I lay in bed, awake. "You will not get me this year," I said quietly to the darkness. "You will not get me next year. You will not get me the year after." One by one I went through the years ahead—eleven, twelve, thirteen, and on—anticipating the coming struggle without even really understanding the enemy.

But even as a kid some part of me knew it was a losing fight. Houdini was my hero: a titan, a giant, a larger-than-life colossus who dreamed of becoming a master magician as a child and then bent the forces of the universe to make it happen. But even he succumbed to this enemy eventually. "My professional life has been a constant record of disillusion," he wrote as an adult—words I highlighted in yellow, seeing them as a warning—"and many things that seem wonderful to most men are the every-day commonplaces of my business."

What is this loss and where does it come from? Though I was too young to recognize it at the time, my interest in magic has been bound to this question from the beginning. As a child I could see some weight in the world pressing down on the adults—parents, teachers, and even, already, some of my friends—and magic was a way to make it go away for a moment. One year at Easter during our annual hunt for plastic eggs I used my newfound sleight-of-hand skills to secretly hide the eggs again as I went around the living room with my younger brother and sister who were still busy trying to find them.

At that age I knew the Easter Bunny wasn't real—I knew my parents had hidden the eggs—and I thought that if I could secretly hide enough of them again my parents would find them and wonder where they had all come from. I wanted to give back some of the mystery and magic they were trying to give us. I thought they needed it more than I did.

That finding wonder and amazement becomes harder as an adult is so universally acknowledged that it sounds obvious. But the more I consider the reason, the less certain I am of a simple explanation.

The common answer goes something like this. As we get older, we learn more about how the world works, and because we have more information, the world becomes less amazing. But logically this doesn't work, and even a child can see it isn't really true. You may learn at school that lightning is a discharge of static electricity built up in the atmosphere and released suddenly into the ground. But this knowledge does nothing to diminish the awesome wonder of a thunderstorm in July that lights up the darkness with incandescent flashes of white spider-webbing across the sky and splits the air with thunder that shakes the walls and sends the cat running for the basement. In the face of this undeniable power it is not the facts about lightning that strike you numb with dread or still with wonder, but rather the direct, immediate experience of those facts. You can explain lightning, but you cannot explain it away.

Wonder is not the product of ignorance. It comes through knowledge rather than in spite of it. In those years of scouring the library shelves for anything even remotely connected to the work of magic and magicians I discovered a passage by Albert Einstein. By this point I had started a notebook of magic—my own magic book—and I copied the quote inside the front cover: "The most beautiful experience we can have is the mysterious. It is the source of all true art and all true science. Whoever does not know it, who can no longer pause to wonder or stand rapt in awe, is as good as dead."

But understanding this is one thing and feeling it is another. I had this quote taped to the inside of my touring case during my first year on the road and I'd read it for inspiration before going onstage. In the beginning it felt like a promise. Then it felt like an accusation. Then it felt like a verdict.

FIVE YEARS IS a long time to be on the road. Even with the six-months-on, six-months-off schedule I had devised to ensure we had as much time together as possible, Katharine and I were tired of the constant time apart. The good shows were better than they had ever been—the pacing was tight and my dynamic range was increasing so I could be funnier in the light moments and more intense in the serious moments, and this gave each performance a depth and a tactility that clearly resonated with the audience. I was signing a lot of posters after each show, and taking a lot of pictures, and it was the only time I had ever really felt like a success. However, I was acting out of character in a way that made me realize something needed to change— skipping sound check, arriving at the airport later and later, almost missing my flights, even forgetting to buy airline tickets to the shows, like if I could just screw this up badly enough I could make it all go away and go home. I knew things were falling apart before they did, giving myself the curious perspective of a captain watching his ship sail toward an iceberg and not knowing how to stop the impending disaster, or whether he even wanted to.

One day I landed at the airport—I think I was in Portland but I couldn't tell you whether it was Maine or Oregon—and texted Katharine from the baggage claim as I waited for my luggage.

Hey. Long day here. Couldn't fall asleep last night and had to wake up at 4 this morning to make the flight. Waiting for my bags now and have no idea how I'm going to get through this one tonight. So tired. Bored. Angry. This is ridiculous. I miss you terribly and wish I could just come home. Be careful what you wish for, right? You might get it. Sorry I'm always so far away. What a fucking mess. Think I need a break from the road for a while. Do you want to run away with me?

A response came back almost immediately.

Hi Nate. Think you intended this for someone else.

Oh shit. My text had not gone to Katharine. My text had gone to the student activities volunteer in charge of my show that night.

How long could this last?

Not long, certainly. Every time I got onstage felt as if it could be the last time, as if this once-grand adventure could all fall apart at any minute, and this gave the shows a desperate, hungry edge that drove them beyond what I was really capable of sustaining as a performer. The result was greatness— sometimes, when it worked—and catastrophe when it didn't. There were no mediocre shows. It was all or nothing. And more and more, it was nothing.

A few nights later in Virginia I got into an argument onstage. I have it on video, actually, and it gets worse every time I watch it. A group of, what—frat guys, athletes?—had been talking to one another throughout the first twenty minutes of the show. Usually I can bring everyone into the fold by the end of the first illusion but that night they kept talking and I lost my patience.

"Hey," I said. "I don't know how to say 'Shut the fuck up' nicely, so I'm just going to say it meanly. Shut the fuck up."

This fell like the first blow in a fistfight. The whole room reeled back, sucker-punched. Everyone sat, silent, still, and waiting. On my good nights I would have listened to this silence carefully, gauging the impact of my words and adjusting my course accordingly, but this wasn't one of my good nights. There may have been an appropriate way to handle this kind of situation, but I hadn't found it. I kept going.

"Listen. I woke up at three in the morning to get here. I care about this. I'm here because I want to be here. What the fuck are *you* doing here?"

Silence. Absolute silence. I knew that my agent was going to get a call about this show. Maybe the campus newspaper was there. Maybe someone was filming this show and I'd be on YouTube by morning. I didn't care.

"If you want to talk to your friends, get the fuck out and go fucking talk to them somewhere else."

They looked at me, shocked but unmoving.

"I'm not joking. You heard me. Get the fuck out."

The four guys stood and shuffled to the exit. They weren't alone. Two girls in the back walked out. Another group of guys did the same. It wasn't a mass defection—most of the audience was still there. It was a bad moment, but it wasn't a disaster.

The disaster came three nights later.

THE BREAK

THAT NIGHT I was scheduled to perform at Marquette University. I arrived in Milwaukee, checked in to the hotel, and drove to the theater early so I could have some time in the room before the show. By that point, the show was more of an argument than an exhibition, and if I didn't bleed out some of that frustration ahead of time, things could get ugly. The janitor let me in the side door and turned on the house-lights. For the moment I had the place to myself so I found a seat halfway back and stared up at the edge of the stage. How would it feel to watch my own show from here in the audience?

Many people can relate to the disillusionment that comes from discovering the grinding day-to-day reality behind the alluring veneer of a job you've always wanted, but this loss carries a special meaning for magicians. A lawyer or a nurse may discover one day that the spark has gone and work that once felt challenging and rewarding has somehow turned to drudgery, but for the magician this is the very heart of the profession that is lost. No one becomes a magician for practical reasons. We get into magic because we love that rush of astonishment and wonder, and when that goes, nothing remains.

⁓

FOUR HOURS LATER I was one hour into a ninety-minute show and it was going spectacularly well. The campus auditorium was packed and I was building to the end of one of my best pieces. A young woman stood next to me onstage—she'd raised her hand to volunteer even before I finished asking for someone to help—and if the next minute or so went well her mind was going to explode.

"Claire," I said, "in just a moment I'm going to ask you to open your hands, but before we go on, let me be clear on one point."

The room was still and everyone was waiting. Claire was listening, motionless, except for her hands, which were stretched out in front of her body and clasped together and almost imperceptibly shaking. She was holding a clear Ziploc bag, sealed and crumpled into a ball inside her fist. She thought it was empty. It was not.

"Before we started I asked you to close your hands around the bag to keep it safe. Do you remember?"

She nodded.

"Since the moment you closed your hands, I haven't been anywhere near you, right? There is no way I could have introduced anything into your hands over the past few minutes?" Now, this wasn't actually true, but it felt true to her and she would remember it that way.

She nodded again.

I turned to the audience. "I had Claire close her hands around the empty bag and I left her here onstage. Then I went down into the audience, borrowed a dollar bill, sealed it inside another Ziploc bag, and asked this gentleman on the other side of the room to hold it closed within his hands. Sir, have I come anywhere near you?" He shook his head. "That's right. I have not." Again, this wasn't true either, but you'd be amazed at the details you can make people forget once you've learned to command their attention.

"Sir, would you remind me of your name?"

"David," he said.

"David, open your hands."

He opened his hands and uncrumpled the bag. It was empty. The audience drew one collective breath, but I held up my hand for them to wait.

"Claire," I said, and then paused to let them get ahead of me so they'd know where I was going. "Open your hands."

I had said those words before. I had said them a thousand times and I would say them a thousand more.

Claire opened her hands and found the dollar sealed inside her Ziploc bag. Her face was bright and the audience was clapping, but I had a weight in the pit of my stomach and I couldn't hear anything. I was staring out above their heads and having a hard time keeping my focus.

"What?" I said.

"That was incredible!" she shouted again.

Something had gone bad. I was standing onstage in front of five hundred people and I had nothing to say. I looked out at the audience and stared up at the stage lights like a deer on the road about to be hit by a car. I couldn't move.

Claire looked at me, expectant. The audience was waiting. How long had I been standing there?

"Claire—ladies and gentlemen—" I said, weakly, and she finally left the stage. The audience was still waiting.

"I just—"

But my mind was wandering.

"I just wanted to say—"

Doing magic used to feel like an adventure. Now I had done this so many times I didn't even need to pay attention. I could just show up and the show would run all on its own. I had moved on, unplugged, disconnected. I was tired of being here. I didn't care anymore. A magician has to believe in the magic or it isn't magic. I was doing all of this for the wrong reasons.

Even from the balcony they could tell something was wrong.

Do you want to know the real secret to becoming a great magician? It's very simple. You just have to care about it more than anyone else would ever consider possible. You give everything inside you to the work, night after night onstage and day after day in the studio or the workshop where you pour your life into the slow, patient job of taking tricks and turning them into magic. The real work happens alone, in front of a mirror practicing for hours on end or in front of a drawing board or a notebook, designing a bridge strong enough to span the great distance between deception on one side and magic on the other. And if you do it right, when you take the stage a show becomes an expression of the absolute highest that you have to offer. Do you want to be a great magician? Anyone can do it. All it takes is your life; your waking, breathing, hoping, hurting, day-in, day-out life.

But something had happened. I had gone back on my end of the bargain. I used to give everything I had to give onstage, as if my whole life hung in the balance. Now it just felt like a job. Somehow all of this had gone wrong.

The room snapped back into focus.

"I need to go," I announced. I was only two thirds of the way through the show.

"I hope you had a good time watching all of this, but I need to go. Good night."

~

THAT NIGHT I sat in the dark in my hotel room and played John Coltrane's *A Love Supreme* as I stared out the second-story window into the parking lot. I saw my rental car below, and across the pavement the hotel sign glowed: FREE WI-FI. HBO. END YOUR DAY THE SUPER 8 WAY.

I wanted to disappear.

I wanted to *actually* disappear. I didn't want it to be a trick. I wanted to vanish.

I tried to call Katharine and it went to voicemail. I left a message at my agency so they wouldn't get blindsided by a call from the university the next morning asking why they got only two thirds of a magic show. Then I looked in the mirror.

When I was young my parents gave me a 1922 silver dollar, and I have carried it with me for almost every show of my life. The coin is heavy and worn. When you balance it on your finger and flick the edge it rings like the sleigh bell in *The Polar Express*. It used to vanish and reappear whenever I performed magic, but now it just comes along in the coin pocket of whatever pants I'm wearing onstage.

In 1922, magic was in its golden age, and Thurston, Dante, Blackstone, and Carter toured the world with their full-evening magic shows. Houdini was at the height of his powers. I wonder how he would be received today. Would Houdini's magic have endured through the years if you could watch it over and over again on YouTube to pick apart his secrets?

I turned on the light and stood in front of the mirror by the flimsy closet door. I held the coin in my left hand and closed my fingers. I opened my hand and it disappeared. I brought it back. I watched the coin vanish over and over, trying to remember how it had felt to make it vanish for the first time.

When was the last time you were truly amazed? For me, it had been quite a while. Somewhere in the rush of show business I had forgotten that the tour is less important than the show, the show less important than the illusion, and the illusion less important than that quiet moment of wonder, which is the reason for doing all of this anyway. I wanted to find it again. I wanted that unfiltered, overpowering astonishment that blinds you, knocks you down, wakes you up, and reminds you that you are alive. I wanted a shiver of the unknown. I wanted to venture past the safety of my convictions and find the wilderness out there beyond the edges of my own world. I wanted to get lost. I wanted an adventure. I wanted a secret door or a buried treasure or something bigger than the world I had found.

Also—frankly—I wanted a second chance. I had reached a point in my life when the clay was beginning to harden and I was unimpressed with my stake in adulthood. I had kept all the wrong parts of childhood and left behind too many of the good ones. I had wanted to become a great magician since I was a boy, but my younger self wouldn't recognize me now: battle-hardened and opportunistic, always maneuvering for the next big break, aiming always at success instead of greatness. You justify it by telling yourself that you're just paying the bills, that one day you'll be ready to turn your attention once again to the craft, the work, the art, forgetting that every day takes you further and further from the artist and the person you want to be. But sometimes you remember. Sometimes during a show you catch a glimpse of whatever it was you were chasing, and that vision of everything you intended to be is enough to lay you low for the rest of the night.

I wanted to stop. I wanted to take everything I'd become as a professional magician and burn it to the ground in one tremendous blaze. And then I wanted go away and dream it all up again the way it should have happened the first time.

IN THE HOURS and hours I spent waiting in airports and sitting on airplanes, I read a lot—fiction, nonfiction, classics, trash, but mostly books about magic. On this particular leg of the tour I'd brought Lee Siegel's *Net of Magic: Wonders and Deceptions in India*. It's an academic text about the legendary street performers of India and the feats of magic that made them famous—snake charming, levitation, fire breathing. It chronicles their performances and the history of magic on the Indian subcontinent, but the best part is the glossy picture insert in the middle, full of haunting black-and-white images of these magicians at work—a cobra rising from a basket, a young man stabbing a skewer through his cheek, an old man sitting cross-legged in a marketplace, his eyes closed, serene, as if unaware that he is floating three feet off the ground.

This did not look like magic in America. These magicians looked like bricklayers or farmers more than entertainers—like working men plying a trade rather than showmen trying to ingratiate themselves to an audience. They showed intensity, urgency, ferocity. I could not stop thinking about these pictures.

And so on that miserable night, as I lay on the bed in my hotel room in Milwaukee, I started paging through the book, looking at the pictures and thinking of this tradition of magic so completely different from my own. I started dreaming of an adventure—a crazy, irresponsible break from the mechanized repetition of touring in America, a quest to the other side of the world to see these things for myself. I wanted to see these magicians with my own eyes. I wanted to feel the way that I used to feel when I watched a magic show and didn't already know the secrets. I didn't want more tricks—I had plenty of tricks. I wanted magic. Real magic.

~

I SOON REALIZED that disappearing to the other side of the world to look for magic would be harder than I thought. For all of the traveling I had done in the United States while on tour, I had no experience with improvised wandering in a foreign country. The places I wanted to go weren't on the main tourist routes, so much of the plan—if you could call my vague intention of making my way across India from east to west by train an actual plan—would be determined as I went. I had the phone numbers of a few local contacts and the email address of a good friend from college already traveling in Asia I could meet along the way, but compared to the bulletproof, clockwork precision of a tour schedule, this was going into uncharted territory.

Running under all of this, too, was my worry that by leaving, I would ruin my career. I had worked my entire life to become

a magician and had finally established a foothold in a notoriously tough profession. After five years of touring on the college
circuit my career had a momentum that could be directed toward
any number of projects. Why let that dissipate? Competition in
the world of entertainment is fierce, and if I disappeared on a
quixotic search for wonder and magic in India there was no guar-
antee that the work would be waiting for me when I came home.

But mostly I thought about Katharine, and that was almost
the end of my interest in India. I had a picture of her I brought
with me on tour, an action shot of her jumping off the couch
holding an electric guitar, mid-howl, and another of her standing
knee-deep in a lake during a canoe trip, covered in mud,
delighted. So much of our time together was remembered, or
anticipated, but precious little just plainly lived. We'd just bought
a house together and I wanted to go home and live in it. The
prospect of going away from her—again, for who knows how
long—was enough to make me want to scrap the whole plan.
I'd go home and talk to her about India, I thought, but was sure
that would be the end of it.

∼

OUR CONVERSATION TOOK three days.

On the first day, we talked about the show in Milwaukee—
the boredom, the anger, and the long frustration of life on the
road. We spoke about money and retirement plans. We argued
and made up and went for a long walk in the woods and talked
about the difference between life as an amateur artist and life as
a professional artist. We talked about creative compromise and
how to truly serve one's craft—is it better to keep money out of
it even if it means working a day job to pay the bills, or is it

better to accept the commercial compromises of professional work so you can spend all of your time working on your art? We argued each side of it and by the end decided it was a lost cause either way. We talked about Houdini and how he had been ready to quit and take a job with the Yale lock company when the famous producer Martin Beck saw him perform and turned him into a superstar. We spoke about how tough it must be to be a superstar.

On the second day we talked about other professions I could take up instead. I loved history, I said, and my years of performing would translate well to a career in the classroom as a history teacher. This became a convenient way to avoid the conversation we should have been having and we spoke of my becoming a teacher as if it was already decided, how I could get a job at the high school up the road from our house and walk to school in the mornings and read in the evenings. If I wanted to keep up with magic I could volunteer at the hospital or give local shows a few times a year. But even as we spoke I knew this approach to magic was impossible. It had always been an all-or-nothing proposition for me. For almost twenty years I had bound myself to the aim and purpose of becoming a great magician, and I had done it so tightly that now I didn't know how to undo it even if I wanted to. I didn't know how to stop, but I didn't know how to keep going, either. The thought of teaching, or any career that would take the place of touring as a professional magician, appealed only in the way you sometimes look down from a high place and love the idea of flying even if it would be the last thing you ever did.

But fooling yourself is easy, and at the moment another job sounded pretty good. That night we built a big fire in the backyard and stayed up late and saw the stars and toasted my new career as a teacher, and we went to bed happy and a little drunk.

"You really would be a magnificent teacher," Katharine said as she was falling asleep. Katharine is one of those people who can use the word "magnificent" and make it mean something.

"Yeah," I said.

"Do you think you could be happy in front of a classroom?" she asked. You could hear the hope in her voice. I was quiet for a long time.

"I think maybe there's more to life than being happy," I finally said, and fell asleep some time later still trying to decide what I meant.

On the third day Katharine had to work, so we didn't get to talk until the evening, but during the day we both realized on our own that I would not become a teacher. When she came home we ate dinner in front of the TV and watched *30 Rock* or *How I Met Your Mother* until the sun had gone down and Katharine suggested we go for a walk.

In Iowa, the fall days are still hot but the nights are cold, and that night the sky was clouded over when we set off on our usual loop. It took us away from the town and along the edge of a park that stretched off on one side and vanished into blackness, punctuated several miles away by the lights from the houses on the other side. The night felt open and wild and larger than life, and as we walked we spoke about the future, and magic, and India.

Katharine and I met in college, and from the beginning she was on board with my work as a magician. This is not to say she *liked* magic or understood why I thought it was so important— for a week or so after we started dating she thought I was really interested in Charles Dickens because I kept going on about David Copperfield—but she knew it mattered to me. After my escape from the river I wanted to do a buried alive stunt—another throwback to Houdini's greatest hits—and when I told her my plan she looked at me directly and asked three questions.

"Do you know how you're going to do it?"

"Yes."

"Have you thought about what might go wrong?"

"I have."

"Have you considered everything you haven't thought about yet?"

"I think so. I won't really know until I get a feel for the ground and the weight of the dirt. At some point I'll just have to dig the hole and find out."

She looked at me again, weighing her answer, I think, and then said, "Okay. Let's go buy some shovels. I'll help you dig."

A friend's parents owned a farm twenty miles out of town and they said I could use their sheep pasture if I promised not to die and also to fill the hole back in when I was done. That afternoon Katharine and I drove to the hardware store and bought two pairs of work gloves and two garden shovels. On the way to the farm we put the windows down in her car and roared the radio like any other college kids out for a drive, but we were on our way to dig a grave to see if I might be able to get out of it after being locked in handcuffs, sealed in a cloth sack, and buried alive. We spent the rest of the day digging, and as we dug she talked about the escape. She had a number of solid objections—the way the weight of the dirt would depend on the rainfall so we couldn't predict how it would actually feel on the day of the performance; the way the audience would want to crowd around the hole to make sure I was really down there and how this might make it hard to hear if something was going wrong and I was calling for help; the way the dirt would crumble under my hands and feet like quicksand as I tried to claw my way to the surface, like swimming in molasses. But as she spoke, she dug, and by the end of the day we had our hole.

"So—what do you think?" Katharine's hair was up in a red handkerchief but a few pieces had escaped and were plastered on her forehead. Her jeans were covered in dirt. We were both soaked in sweat and had collapsed on the grass by the edge of the grave.

"I don't think I can do it," I said.

"Yeah, I came to the same conclusion," she said. "But really, it's not that you *couldn't* do it. You'd probably be fine. You just couldn't be sure. And," she added, "it would be a really stupid way to die."

"Are you sore we spent all day digging out here?"

She laughed. "Are you kidding? This was the greatest day in a long time. Who gets to hang out with sheep and dig in the dirt as a grown-up?"

~

WE TURNED OFF the main road and down a path that would take us home through the forest. I had been silent for a long time.

"Hey," Katharine said. "Are you really going to go to India?"

"I don't know."

"Can I tell you what I think?"

"God, yes. Please."

"I think you should do it."

"Why?"

She stopped walking. "You used to be so much fun. You're so serious now."

"I'm still fun," I said.

"No you're not. Why don't you do magic at home anymore?"

"Because I hate it now."

"Do you want to keep doing magic?"

"I don't know."

"Do you want to do anything else?"

"No."

"Okay. Well, you should probably go away and figure out what you're going to do, then."

She didn't talk for a few minutes.

"How long are you going to be gone?"

PART TWO

HOW TO DISAPPEAR

EVERYONE HAD TOLD me about the heat. They were right. The heat was extraordinary. I could feel it on the plane even before they opened the airplane door, overwhelming the air conditioning in the cabin as we taxied to the gate. Once I stepped outside the airport it was hard to think of anything else. Dust and thick black car exhaust choked the air, and everywhere the sounds of cars honking, brakes screeching, drivers shouting, and engines running hot overpowered any possibility of rational thought. For a moment I didn't move, stunned and disoriented. In a distant part of my mind I wondered vaguely what I should do—find a ride, find a hotel, move from here to somewhere else. But high above, the late-afternoon sun shone relentlessly down on all of us, and mostly I just stood there and endured the heat.

An hour later, I sat on the curb at the side of a road in Kolkata, trying to figure out what to do and worrying that I'd made a terrible mistake. The bright yellow 1930s-era taxi that had brought me there from the airport had just driven away. To my right, two children and a dog picked through a pile of garbage. I faced a row of two-story buildings, their tops bristling with snarls of electrical wiring and their brick façades in various states of decay. Behind them lay the entire subcontinent of India. I was hot, tired, stricken senseless with jet lag, and reeling from the realization that I had left everything—family, job, friends, the rest of the world—behind. My home in Iowa City, Iowa, was almost as far from this patch of sunbaked concrete as you could get. The shortest distance home passed through the center of the earth.

Sudder Street was known as the backpackers' district in Kolkata but I didn't see any other backpackers. I had never seen squalor and destitution like this before. A young boy held a naked infant and sat on a blanket against one of the buildings. A man had been lying facedown on the sidewalk near the gutter since I arrived. He hadn't moved. A woman in bright orange and red crouched at the edge of the street. I couldn't tell what she was doing. A goat walked by. Something was burning.

I am overprivileged. This poverty was worse than I had ever even begun to imagine. The majesty and the mystery of this adventure, so clear and urgent in the days leading up to departure, had gone. I wanted to go home.

"You are American?"

A man approached. I couldn't tell if he was closer to fifty or seventy. He had short black hair and a gray beard and wore a faded red shirt with a blue cloth wrapped around his waist. I didn't want to talk to anyone. I didn't know what to do. I nodded.

"I am Ahmed." He put his hand on his chest and repeated his name. "Ahmed."

"Hello, Ahmed."

He asked if I had a hotel. I did not.

"Come with me. I will show you a good hotel."

Now that I was here I wasn't sure how I intended to simply show up and find a place to stay, but following a strange man through this burned-out neighborhood was not how I imagined the afternoon playing out. I shook my head.

"Come with me. I will show you a good hotel. Safe." He pointed down the street.

Ahmed looked stern and serious and made no effort to curry favor or trust, which I took as an immeasurably good sign. I did need a place to stay and I couldn't have been the first American to stumble stunned and disoriented out of a cab into the backpackers' district of Kolkata. I stood up and shouldered my bag.

Ahmed walked down the road and I followed. The streets were paved but covered in dust that billowed into the air as cars and rickshaws passed, catching the light from the setting sun and making it feel like a scene from a well-lit movie about the end of the world. A group of men sat on plastic stools at a tea stand and watched me pass.

Ahmed stopped in front of a one-story brick building with a small metal door and a sign that said GUESTHOUSE. He turned to me.

"This is a good hotel."

It did not look like a good hotel. It looked like the back door to a butcher shop. I wanted Ahmed to go away. I wanted to open my bag and dig out the guidebook and find the name of an overpriced, unapologetically luxurious hotel and go there and take a shower and sleep like the dead. I did not feel like a good person. I wanted to use the two credit cards and three hundred dollars in cash I had in my back pocket to escape this place and go back to my home where children and dogs did not eat from the same pile of garbage. I was tired and ashamed of my revulsion.

I reached into my pocket for some money, intending to tip Ahmed so he would go away. Then, for some reason that I don't entirely understand—maybe the look on Ahmed's face or the uneasy feeling I was getting from this "hotel"—I hesitated.

Ahmed looked down at my handful of change. I had gotten the coins in the airport and was holding them in my open hand. I noticed that the Indian five-rupee coin was about the same size as a U.S. quarter. Without even really thinking about it, I put the rest of the coins back into my pocket.

Ahmed looked up at me, and then back down at the coin. My fingers did their dance. The coin vanished.

Ahmed lost it.

Everyone should learn and perform one great magic trick. In the reactions of the audience you see a side of humanity almost completely hidden during the rest of day-to-day life, and the world would be a better place if everyone could witness this at least once. From the students on the playground at recess to this man named Ahmed who worked in a terrible neighborhood in Kolkata, the response to great magic is the same: a mouth stunned open, widening eyes, fear, doubt, and then openly, nakedly, joy. Pure joy. This transformation is far, far more amazing than the trick, which is just a tool designed to create this moment. A moment of pure astonishment makes you forget to be cool. It makes you forget to be composed or distinguished. It makes you forget to—consciously—be anything. The faces that are revealed when our masks of self-awareness and propriety are blasted away are, simply, beautiful. Magicians get to see people at their best. I wish everyone could have this experience.

Ahmed was beside himself. He laughed. He put his arm on my shoulder. He kept laughing. His wife was just down the street—could I show the coin going away to her? Also, his brother was not very far off—could he see it, too? In that one moment everything changed and I was no longer just a tourist.

When magic is bad it is worse than almost anything. When it is good it becomes a way to see a side of humanity that is the same in all of us, a way to find, in astonishment, the common ground that bridges political, economic, geographic, cultural, and religious differences, a window through which we can see that despite everything, we are not as different as we imagine.

I checked in to the hotel. The room was small but surprisingly clean for the state of the building. I had been awake for almost two days. At home in Iowa the sun was just rising.

~

I HAD STRANGE dreams that night—of Katharine and home, of life on the road in America, and the common nightmare among magicians of wandering into a room in your house and discovering a theater filled with people waiting for your show to begin. I slept badly and woke early, staring at the unfamiliar curtain across the window as the reality of the situation slowly resolved itself into clarity.

I was in India.

Outside, the whine of a two-stroke engine broke the early-morning silence as a rickshaw driver began his day. This woke a dog, who began barking, and over the next twenty minutes the whole city came to life. The gray light from the window illuminated the room—my bag in the sink, up off the floor to keep it away from the cockroaches.

There was a knock at the door. Andy was here.

I first met Andy in college. He was the student body president and gave pie-making lessons at a local cooking store. This combination, along with his massive Friday night dinner parties, made him something of a local celebrity. If you didn't know him personally, you had heard of him.

Andy had helped start an underground nonprofit organization called the James Gang. No one really knew who they were or what they did, but every few weeks something great would take place in town—a concert, a festival, the grand opening of a new art gallery space—and at the bottom of the poster or invitation you would see "A James Gang Endeavor" and know that Andy and his mysterious posse of poets and artists had struck again. They had apparently convinced a number of local bankers and business owners that the best way to foster an environment of creativity and culture in a college town out in the middle of the cornfields was to give money to the James Gang to fund these projects. It worked. We had more poetry readings, art shows, independent film screenings, concerts, and music festivals per capita than anywhere for a thousand miles in any direction. And Andy was at the center of it all.

When I was a freshman in college I would practice new material by going down to the Ped Mall—eight square blocks in downtown Iowa City blocked off from car traffic—to do street magic for people: students, construction workers, homeless people, anyone. One afternoon, after watching for a while, a guy maybe two or three years older than I handed me a business card and said, "You do good work. We would like to help. Drop us an email and we'll find a time to sit down and talk about how we can work together."

Then he walked away.

I looked down at the business card, which was printed on thick, translucent vellum. One side was blank except for an email address in small black letters along one edge. The other side simply read THE JAMES GANG.

Since that day I have collaborated with Andy on every major project I have ever done. That initial contact led to a run of shows in a performance venue that the James Gang had recently opened above a bar downtown. This weekly show—and the new material I had to generate each week to fill it—effectively put an end to any chance of success I had as a student but taught me almost everything I needed to know about being a magician. A few years later we produced a DVD of my first college tour.

Everyone assumed that after college Andy would go to Hollywood and become a film director or to Washington to get into politics: he had been accepted to the USC film school and already had a job offer from someone on the Hill. But Andy didn't go to Hollywood and he didn't go to Washington. "I want to change the world," he explained just before selling all of his possessions, breaking his lease, and disappearing for four years, "but I have never seen it. I have to go see it first."

Over the next four years Andy traveled the world and embarked on a series of increasingly incredible adventures. He taught English in a small village in China, appeared in three Bollywood films, and worked for a nonprofit NGO in Burma. He collaborated on documentaries for ESPN and National Geographic and hosted a cooking special on Armenian National Television about the American Thanksgiving holiday in which he roasted a turkey, cooked stuffing, and baked pumpkin pie in the kitchen of the American embassy on live TV. He lived in a Buddhist monastery in Korea, a mud hut in rural South Africa, and a tiny fishing village in India. And he has the photos—and in the case of the Bollywood films, the DVDs—to prove it. It's amazing.

Along the way, Andy had been making no-budget documentaries about the people he met. When I wrote to tell him about my trip, he was working as a line cook at a truck stop in the middle of the Australian outback. I laid out the plan of traveling across India and he said he'd like to come along for the adventure. "We'll make a documentary about your search for magic in another culture," he said. "Like Anthony Bourdain traveling the world to explore the cuisine of other countries, but with magic."

We had a few rules. First, the trip would always come before the filming. I would go to India and do what I intended to do, and Andy would come along and film whatever he wanted. There would be no staging scenes for the camera, and if the camera ever got in the way of the adventure, we'd put it away and forget about it.

However, there were concessions. I agreed to wear a little radio mic sometimes so Andy's camera could hear whatever I said, and some of the places I wanted to go required permission to film, which would have to be worked out along the way.

Andy walked into the room. In one hand he held a paper bag. "Breakfast," he said, and held it toward me. In the other hand he was balancing two shot-glass-sized terracotta cups, steaming and filling the room with the scent of anise and cloves. It smelled like actual salvation. "This is chai," Andy said, "and it's one of the greatest beverages in the world." He handed one to me and raised his cup in a toast. "Welcome to India."

KOLKATA

THE HEAT CAME early in the day and by lunchtime the air was heavy and hot. I was losing my battle with jet lag and thinking mostly of coffee. The booksellers lining Bankrim Chatterjee Street looked up distractedly from their own reading to hawk new textbooks and old paperback novels from their open-air stalls as we passed. The street was filled with students in collared shirts from the nearby college and older women in yellow-and-orange saris holding umbrellas to block out the sun. Motorcycles wove between the pedestrians and an all-white 1940s-era Studebaker made a path through the crowd by sounding its horn until people gave way. Everywhere, something smelled delicious.

Ten minutes later we were installed at a table in the Indian Coffee House in the old Albert Hall building. The room was as large as a school gymnasium and looked as if it was built at the height of the British raj, with molded plaster ceilings stretching forty feet above us and a battalion of ornate wrought-iron fans suspended overhead, spinning silently but struggling to circulate the air. Waiters in crisp white uniforms and white caps hurried drinks on silver trays from the kitchen to the tables.

One of them brought a small glass of water and a cup of thick, perfect, life-giving coffee—dark, potent, and syrupy with sugar—and I was so relieved to see the coffee that I thanked him with what must have been alarming fervor. "Is okay, sir," he said with his hands up as he backed slowly away. Inside I could feel my humanity creeping back from the brink. Arteries dilated, blood rushed to my brain, my heart swelled with love for everything. I sat for a moment to drink the water and sip the coffee and the world settled back down again.

The room was full. I think we found the last unoccupied table, and most were crowded with middle-aged men and women leaning in and speaking intently, deep in conversation. I wondered if we had interrupted them—most of the tables had ceased their conversations and turned to look in our direction. I suspected this place didn't get tourists very often. I leaned back in my chair and drank my coffee. I liked it here tremendously.

"Hey, I have a picture to show you," Andy said. He swung his backpack to the ground and pulled a photo from between the pages of a book. He handed it to me. "It's from Zambia."

A woman, her mouth open, eyes wide and bright, beamed out at me from beneath a yellow headscarf. She was sitting cross-legged on the ground in a mud-hut village and maybe a dozen other women sat around her, staring at a rubber band stretched between her two index fingers. Everyone was laughing. I knew that look.

"That's the rubber band trick," I said. Before Andy left on his trip around the world I taught him one of my very first magic tricks, a simple illusion with two rubber bands in which one appears to melt seamlessly through the other. It's beginner's-level magic but the visual moment of the illusion is so perfect that you don't even need to say anything, you just do it. I thought it would be a good way to communicate if you didn't speak the local language, a useful tool for a traveler headed out into the world. You never know when you'll need to be amazing.

"I have done that trick so many times," Andy said. "I've performed it for a group of sheepherders in Tibet, a biker gang in Australia, a group of students who were trying to climb Mount Kilimanjaro—everywhere. I was sitting on a bench at a bus stop in Korea and this old man sat down next to me and began to read a newspaper. I started doing the rubber band trick over and over, and after a minute he put down the newspaper and said 'Again!' So I did it again, and he just looked at me without saying anything for fifteen seconds. Then he asked if I had been traveling for long, and where I had been, and then he asked if I wanted to join him for tea."

"Wow," I said.

"It would not have happened without the rubber band trick. It's the most extraordinary way to connect with people. Speaking of connecting with people, we should talk about the trip."

"What do you mean?"

"Well, you said in your email that you were on a quest for wonder. Who talks like that, by the way? You're the only person on the planet who still talks about going on quests. So—we're looking for wonder."

"Yeah."

"What do you mean?"

"What do you mean, 'what do you mean?' We're looking for magic."

"You came to India to find magic shows and watch them?"

"Yes. Well, kind of. I want to feel like that lady in your picture."

Andy took the two rubber bands off his wrist and began to perform the rubber band trick.

"Shut up," I said. "You know what I mean."

We ordered lunch and made a plan to move west by train, first to Varanasi that night, and we would figure the rest out as we went.

Varanasi appealed to me for two reasons. First, I had heard it was famous for its snake charmers and I wanted to find one. Snake charming stood at the crossroads of my lifelong love of magic and lifelong aversion to snakes, and just the thought of it held a sort of power over me. Second, Varanasi was a convenient stop-off on an east-to-west crossing of India by train, and an overnight train meant we didn't have to pay for a hotel.

"I'd really like to find these guys," I said, and slid my copy of *Net of Magic* across the table. Andy picked up the book and flipped through the pages, stopping at the photo section in the middle.

"That's incredible," he said.

"I know. They're a tribe of street magicians who live in a slum outside New Delhi. I sent an email to the author before I left to see if he could set up an introduction."

After we ate, I absentmindedly took a deck of cards from my bag and began flipping them back and forth between my hands. The instinct to practice at any possible moment is deeply ingrained in most magicians and few leave home without a deck of cards in case a few spare moments open up during the day. A friend of mine was working on a coin trick and got into the habit of hiding a coin in his hand all day long—while driving, showering, eating, everywhere—so during a performance he could conceal it behind his fingers in a natural manner.

I flicked the cards off the top of the deck from one hand to another.

"Excuse me, sir!" Our waiter was back, flanked by two others. "Gambling is strictly prohibited in our coffeehouse. Please to put the cards back in your knapsack."

"Oh, what? Sorry. I'm not gambling. I'm doing magic."

This didn't impress them, and he told me again to put the cards away.

"Even if I'm not gambling?" A few of the other tables turned to look at us again, disapproving and irritated.

"Sir, please to put them away."

We got up to leave, but as we approached the door a group of students turned to get our attention and a young man of about twenty raised his hand. "Excuse me, please." We walked over.

"You are American?" the young man asked. He wore an Adidas track jacket and dark-rimmed glasses. They all had notebooks out on the table but when we approached they cleared them to the side to make room and invited us to sit.

"They are very sensitive about playing cards here," he explained. "A few years ago there was a great deal of gambling here and they have worked hard to make this a place of discussion and debate once again."

I thanked him for the explanation. "I just assumed they didn't want visitors."

He waggled his head from side to side. Later I would learn that this uniquely Indian gesture translates loosely to "I recognize what you are saying and am responding without agreeing or disagreeing with you," but at the moment I didn't know how to respond. One of the students asked why I had come to

India and I told him I was there to learn about magic. They hadn't expected this.

"In this country we believe everything has a scientific explanation," a young woman said. "If we see a magician, we know there is a specific method he is using to make his tricks."

"Do you believe in magic?" I asked. I'm not sure what I mean when I ask people this question, but it's a way to get them to start talking about a subject that would otherwise require a great deal of conversational buildup.

"No," said the woman. "Yes," said the man in the track jacket. "We don't see the ghosts, but we believe. When we hear ghost stories, we get the goose bumps."

"Yes, we do believe in mysteries," added another student, this one wearing a green Megadeth T-shirt.

"Everything has a scientific explanation," insisted the woman, "even if we don't understand the science."

~

I AM NOT the first magician from the Western world to travel to India in search of magic. India has long had a reputation for being a place where magic might actually be real. The travel poster promoting Indian tourism in O'Hare airport featured a picture of the Taj Mahal and the words INDIA: A LAND OF MYSTERY.

The country's ancient tradition of magic is well known but little understood in the world of magicians. I knew, for instance, that one of the pieces in my own show had its roots in the work of these traditional magicians—that it had originated in India, made its way to Europe, then to America, and was then picked up by Houdini and made famous. I liked the idea of tracing my

own art back to its beginnings, and I imagine that other magicians have had the same idea. In general, magicians love to be
amazed. After years of perfecting the craft, the experience of
being genuinely astonished by another magician's work is so
rare that if someone is doing something that can't be explained,
other magicians will go to great lengths and travel great distances
to see it for themselves.

In 1899, at the height of the British Empire, Charles Bertram
left behind a successful career as the favorite magician of
England's King Edward VII to explore the magic of the Indian
subcontinent. "There comes a time in the life of every man
when he wishes to enlarge the field of his operations," he wrote
afterward, "and having decided that this was desirable in my
own case, my thoughts naturally turned to the East, which from
time immemorial has been steeped in the fascinating tradition
of the Black Art." In his memoirs he makes the curiously specific
claim that he witnessed 106 performances during his time in
India, and he described many of the illusions that have become
synonymous with traditional Indian street magic.

Around this same time, the famous American illusionist
Harry Kellar traveled through India and sought out performances by as many traditional Indian magicians as he could find.
Before I left for India I came across the account of his adventures,
A Magician's Tour Up and Down and Round About the Earth, and
read about magic too impossible to believe. One afternoon a
snake charmer visited Kellar in his hotel room. When the snake
charmer played his flute—on the opposite side of the room—
Kellar "saw the sheet on the bed rise up till it looked like a small
tent, and then an enormous cobra crawled out and coiled itself
on the floor." Later, he described a bloody street performance

in which the magician massacred a young boy with a sword and then brought him back to life.

In the years to come, dozens of magicians from the West descended on India in search of the infamous Indian Rope Trick. The accounts of this illusion varied in certain specifics, but the general premise was the same. A magician walked to the center of an open field, placed a basket on the ground, and began to play a flute. As he played, a rope rose from the basket and continued into the air, unsupported, until it stretched into the sky. The magician's young assistant would then climb the rope, and either he would disappear into thin air at the top or, in some more violent versions of the story, the magician would climb after the young boy carrying a sword clenched between his teeth and the illusion would end as the severed and bleeding limbs, head, and broken body of the boy fell from the sky back to the earth. In some versions of the story the magician would then magically restore the boy to life.

The Indian Rope Trick was a sensation, and magicians around the world launched a campaign to find someone who could perform it. None of them succeeded, of course, and in his extraordinary book *The Rise of the Indian Rope Trick*, Peter Lamont pulls back the curtain on this long-standing hoax. In 1890 the *Chicago Tribune* published an anonymous account of the illusion, complete with a photograph of the Indian magician purported to have accomplished the impossible feat. The story was a runaway hit and the illusion became legendary, but there was a problem—the reporter had invented the entire article. The illusion was never performed. Four months later the paper printed a retraction of the story, but by then it had spread throughout the Western world and has been repeated for more than a hundred years.

None of this prevented the grand stage illusionists of America and Europe from inventing their own versions of the famous Indian Rope Trick. Thurston staged the illusion every night in his live theater show. So did Blackstone. The illusion had captured the imagination of the West, and India has been known ever since as a land of magic and mystery.

KOLKATA'S HOWRAH TRAIN station towered above the surrounding neighborhood like a prison, with stout brick walls and blockhouse towers defending every corner. Inside the gloomy, cavernous interior an entire village of destitute children begged the travelers for coins and an army of bustling station attendants in blue uniforms hurried past and pretended not to see them. We began our search for tickets and waited for an hour at the Computerized Reservation Office only to meet a man whose job appeared to be to tell people that they have waited in the wrong line. It took another hour and a progression of offices and service windows, but finally we had what we wanted—two tickets on the overnight train to Varanasi.

The train didn't leave until later that evening, so Andy and I had the rest of the day to explore the city. Fortified by the coffee and the successful navigation of the ticket office, I was beginning to feel as if I had a grip on this new place, but we found an outdoor market that reminded me how far I was from home. Vendors stretched down both sides of the road and sold cloth, jewelry, flowers, fruit, cell phones, candles, everything—some stacked neatly on stands or carts and others piled haphazardly on the ground. One merchant used a machete to hack open fresh green coconuts so you could drink the milk before scooping the soft meat out from inside. Another squatted on the road behind a metal pail filled with eggs and held a cardboard sign announcing PICO'S EGG SHOP. Dogs and goats wandered freely, children slept under carts as their parents worked above, and everywhere the scent of dust, gasoline, incense, spice, roasting meat, and humanity mixed together into a smell I would come to associate closely with India as the trip went on but struck me in that moment as new and overpowering. A man about my age pushed a bicycle covered with living chickens through the market, their feet gathered and bound together in two unhappy bunches— one at the front of the bike and one at the back—all clucking and screeching as he offered them up for sale. Andy saw my revulsion at this. "Nate, look around you. How else are you going to keep them fresh?"

At a bookseller's stand I found a notebook. I had been looking for one, thinking I would probably want to record some of the trip along the way, and this one was perfect. Inside it had fresh blank pages, but the leather-bound cover looked aged and worn, as though it had already been through a few good stories and somehow ended up here ready for another. It looked like a book about magic: old and mysterious, like something out of Indiana Jones. I bought it from the merchant along with a few books.

Later that evening when we sat at the station waiting to board our train I opened the notebook and wrote a question at the top of the first page: *Where do you find wonder?* This was the central question for a magician, certainly, but I also thought it was an important question for anyone. Wonder is something that everyone cares about but no one discusses, and I probably wasn't the only one in my generation to lie awake in bed one night, unable to sleep, trying to figure out when everything had gone so numb and how to get back. *Where do you find wonder?* is a good question, but it carries an unstated assumption. The real question is, *Where do you find wonder after you have lost it?* That's what I wanted to learn on this trip—why you lose it, and how you get it back.

I knew this: whatever it was, wonder had nothing to do with the Mickey Mouse, Hallmark-card, stars-and-sparkles associations it had back home. In America, and maybe in the West in general, "wonder" had largely been ceded to the realm of children's entertainment and sentimentality. Adults—the thinking went—preferred diversion, edification, and distraction: football, gin, Netflix, GQ magazine, craft beer, politics, wood-fired pizza, Facebook, mystery novels, and horror films. Adults talk about essentially everything except wonder. This exclusion was so complete that it couldn't be accidental. Why?

I had one last thought before boarding the train. My original plan had been to seek out the magicians in India and let their work amaze me, but now this felt roundly inadequate and naive. In just over twenty-four hours here I had seen enough to recognize that while the magic in India might be good—and I hoped it was—the country itself was astonishing. That evening we had come in to the station over the massive Howrah Bridge, which sweeps you from street level high up through the air and suddenly you can see for miles, with all of Kolkata below you and the whole of India stretching out to the horizon. When we crossed, the sun was dropping lower and the cool blue of the sky was already turning yellow and orange. It had been a long time since I'd noticed a sky like that one.

I looked up from my notebook after I'd scrawled down these ideas. An old man staggered slowly down the platform and then stopped and stood still, looking up to the high windows where the same evening sun cut through the gloom of the station. He stood there for a moment, tottering, alone in his destitution. Then, slowly, the weight of his frail, failing body overcame him and he sat down gingerly, then crumpled to the floor, resting his head on the concrete and keeping his face turned toward the light above. His eyes were still open but he didn't move much. A train had come in and passengers stepped around and over him. A woman bent down to him and he growled something and she hurried away. He lay there fending off the occasional offer of aid and all the time looking up at the window. I don't know if he ever got up again. India was beauty and suffering, side by side, over and over.

THE TRAIN TO VARANASI

THAT EVENING THE train pulled away from Howrah station and I watched through the window as the fortress of red brick and bureaucracy disappeared behind us. I was not sorry to see it go. As we set off, the light from the setting sun flashed and flickered between the buildings, faster and faster, and Varanasi loomed somewhere ahead. Through the window, I could see backyards, back doors, and side streets before they fell away and all that remained of Kolkata was a pack of children racing along the tracks, waving to the departing train. One raised a stick above her head like a sword and ordered us off to battle. I returned the salute. Then they were gone.

Andy sat down next to me.

The bench across from us was empty, but farther down the car an Indian family occupied both sides of the aisle. The daughter sat on the floor, singing a high, playful rhyme in an unfamiliar language. The mom wore a bright yellow sari and unloaded food wrapped in aluminum foil from a paper grocery sack. It smelled delicious. Andy pulled his bag from under the seat and produced two bottles of beer. This was a minor miracle. We had been together all day, and I had no idea when or where he'd found them, or how he'd kept them cold, but I didn't question my good fortune.

An older couple sat on the other end of the car, watching us. Or, rather, they were watching Andy, who'd taken out his camera and was filming the countryside. Andy is something of a paradox. His clothes—duct-taped sandals, a ragged black T-shirt near the end of its useful life, and a tired pair of camping pants that zipped off at the knee—gave him the appearance of a vagabond, but his camera easily cost more than five thousand dollars and he changed the lens and framed his shot with the patient, deliberate care of a Zen master. This piqued their interest, and they sidled over for a better look.

"Can you see anything out there?"

The man spoke with a British accent and wore a gray wool jacket. The woman stood behind him, beaming, eyebrows raised, and I suddenly worried they were going to sell us something. They slid into the bench across from us.

Andy stopped recording and raised his beer bottle in greeting. "Just the end of the sunset."

The couple—I guessed they were in their sixties—were from Birmingham and nearing the end of a six-week exploration of India by train. They had started in Mumbai and traveled south through Goa to Kerala before working their way up the east coast of India to Kolkata. The woman worked as a schoolteacher and the man had worked in sales for a number of years with a firm in London. We learned all this in about thirty seconds.

He asked what I did for a living.

This is a hard question for magicians. I feel a kinship with poets, painters, musicians, writers, and everyone else who holds an occupation that, when shared with strangers, is met with an incredulous and only sometimes unspoken *"And you can make a living at that?"* To answer is to be immediately misunderstood. When I'm on tour in America I tell the most outrageous lies to those who breach the outer defenses of dark sunglasses and headphones that I wear on airplanes. In these cases I am an architect. Cathedrals, exclusively. I am a cathedral architect. Or a teacher. Or a professor. Of quantum physics. I'm on my way to Boston to deliver a lecture on hydrostatic thermonuclear game theory at MIT.

But here my guard was down. "I'm a magician," I said to the man on the train, and immediately felt like an idiot. He raised his eyebrows.

"You're a what?"

"I'm a magician. I do magic."

The woman's eyes grew wide. She nodded and said, "Oh, that's fun!"

The man frowned. "And you can make a living at that?"

I hated both of these people. "Yes, indeed."

The man was winding up for a monologue and not really listening. His capacity for ignoring wonders was itself a marvel; outside, the sun was setting—perfectly, gorgeously—but he continued speaking.

"We went to Las Vegas several years ago and saw a magic show. What was his name?" His wife didn't remember. "For his first joke—that's what you call them, right? Jokes? Or tricks?"

Another brief mid-story conference with his wife failed to resolve this uncertainty.

"There was a table, a box, and a lady. And the joke was that he would disappear and then appear in the box. But the whole thing was so obvious."

The sun had set completely and the haunting, ethereal light from the window had been replaced with a flat and empty black that reflected the image of this small, ridiculous man who stole my sunset.

He kept talking. "Anyway, the whole show was actually quite dull." He hesitated and looked at me expectantly, wondering if he had convinced me that I should retire from my profession right there in the train car and take up another line of work before we reached Varanasi. Earlier in the day I might have tried to change his mind, but now I was enjoying the hum of the train over the tracks and the taste of the beer and the knowledge that the dark, empty space just beyond this man's reflection in the window was *India*, of all places, and that I was on a real adventure.

"Have you been to Varanasi before?" Andy can be very polite.

"Me? No. It's supposed to be the holiest city in India. I've heard that people swim in the Ganges River every morning because they think it's sacred. I'm not getting in that river, but I'll take a look at it and watch *them* swim."

I stared straight ahead, stunned that the Western world's cheap perception of magic that I had worked so hard to escape had followed me here to India and now sat across from me on the train. I was no longer listening. I was somewhere outside in this dark land, watching the train fly through the night.

I GOT UP to explore the train and as I walked past the family at the other end of the car the father raised his hand to catch my attention. A teacher, I thought, or maybe a professor. He was in his midforties and wore a cream linen shirt and gold-rimmed glasses.

"Excuse me, please. You are a magician?" He must have heard me speaking to the man from Birmingham.

I nodded. He shook my hand and motioned for me to sit.

"What is the nature of the magic that you do?" He spoke with a hyper-articulate, lilting clarity.

"Would you like to see something?" I asked him.

One of my favorite illusions is a number-reading effect. First, you write a number on a piece of paper and crumple it in my hand without showing anyone. Then you ask the spectator to name a number between one and a hundred, and when they do, it ends up matching the number written at the beginning. It's a simple piece of magic, but it's very effective because the moment of astonishment happens in the minds of the spectators rather than in front of their eyes. It's sleight of mind rather than sleight of hand, and this internal experience—maybe more than any purely visual moment of magic—feels truly impossible.

The mom let out a surprised hoot. The man with the gold-rimmed glasses looked at the floor and slowly nodded.

"Why do you do this?"

"I love magic."

"And this is 'magic' to you?"

"I would say that this is a way for me to see magic."

"That is very, very interesting. Now, I have to tell you that I know that what you are doing is a trick. I do not know how you are doing this trick, but I have watched magicians before and I always know '*That is a trick*.'"

He said this so directly and with such total lack of hostility or smugness that I didn't know how to respond. I had dealt with as many belligerent, drunken frat guys, cross-armed arch-skeptics, and unimpressible boyfriends as the next magician. But this man wasn't heckling me.

"May I tell you something?" He looked concerned.

"Of course."

"You must know that there is a difference between tricks," he said, pointing to my hands, "and the actions performed by the mental power." He pointed to his head. "You are doing tricks but you say that you are a magician. You are pretending that your tricks are magic. But they are not magic. They are empty. They are nothing. Worthless." Then, realizing that this total damnation of my entire career could be perceived as an insult, he added, "Don't take my words as some abuse—"

But I cut him off. "I don't understand. All magicians do tricks."

"The actions performed by real mental power and real mental strength are different than tricks."

"So you're telling me that there are things that look like magic that aren't actually a trick, but rather the result of . . ."

"Yes. Of mental power." He looked at me as if this should settle everything.

"You'll forgive me for finding this hard to believe."

He straightened. "I have experienced these things myself. And I will tell you a recent example."

I couldn't believe that I was having this conversation.

The man continued. "I was traveling to Agra with my sister. Another woman who we did not know was sitting on a bench across from us and she kept staring at my sister for ten or fifteen minutes. Suddenly my sister started feeling *thirst*, so she drank from a bottle of water and then fainted. She lost consciousness. I was very worried, so I questioned the woman—because I thought that she had done something to my sister—and the woman chanted some words and my sister regained consciousness. But she is still under the effect of that power. Two months have gone by and she is still feeling very weak. So that is just a simple incident that I have come across."

"And you attribute that woman's power to . . ."

"Superior mental strength. Yes."

He told this story without the least effort toward drama or suspense and succeeded in making the casting of a malicious spell sound like a trip to the grocery store. I was torn between the assumption that this man was insane and the evidence— namely, his polite, well-dressed, respectable-looking family and his careful, deliberate way of speaking—that he was not.

"Let me say it this way," he continued. "If you ask a five-year-old boy 'What is two times two?' he may be able to answer 'Four.' You may ask a ten-year-old boy 'What is twenty times thirteen?' and he could give you the correct answer of 260. As unlikely as it sounds, you may even be able to find a person who can answer you if you ask 'What is 555 multiplied by 465?' It might look impossible. You might call that a trick because you don't know how to calculate such a large figure. But is it a trick? No. That is not a trick. That is superior mental strength."

I pointed out that the ability to solve math problems is hardly the same as casting a hex on someone's sister.

"Why? Why is it different?" He spoke without anger or even reprimand. "You might assume that it is different because it is beyond your mental power, but multiplication seems impossible for a child who has only learned addition and subtraction."

He put one hand to his chest. "I am a student of science. I have done my education in physics. I am a computer hardware specialist and I have a degree in computer science as well. I tell you this so you know the scientific world in which I live. I have come across such experiences that make me believe that there are things in this world that don't have any answer. It is difficult to accept because they are so strange in nature; they are so unacceptable at first sight; they are so effective in making you a believer. I know that the woman used her power on my sister. I have seen it."

I looked at him with what must have been an insulting combination of awe and incredulity.

"All of the knowledge that we have accumulated is only a tiny portion of the total available knowledge. Here is knowledge," he said, holding his hands close together and indicating the space between. Then he spread his arms wide. "The rest is mystery. There is so much yet to be discovered."

I WANTED TO believe this man's story about the spell, but a few nonmagical explanations came immediately to mind—heat stroke, dehydration—the sister was thirsty, after all. But more disarming than the story was the quiet, unaffected certainty of the man as he told it. *Oh, you want directions to the mall? Sure, it's just two miles down the road on your left. You want to hear about magic? One time a woman cast an evil spell on my sister, and she's still suffering the consequences. No big deal.*

Andy had disentangled himself from the Birmingham couple and had somehow produced two sandwiches, two bags of potato chips, and two more bottles of beer that sat waiting when I rejoined him on our bench. I told him about my conversation, and Andy could tell that the two encounters—first with the

British man who thought magic was too frivolous and then with the Indian man who thought it was too serious—had unseated my sense of purpose.

"Nate, I've spent a lot of time in India. It can be very difficult to tell what is real and what is fake, and I want you to just consider the possibility that maybe this isn't the most important distinction. You met a man who actually believes that someone cast a spell on his sister. The fact that a well-educated, articulate adult believes in spells seems far more interesting than the question of whether or not spells actually exist."

This wasn't helping. I stood, but Andy offered one final thought.

"Whether or not his story is actually true is beside the point. Isn't it possible that belief in spells makes them real? Isn't that the entire basis for hypnotism? People think it works, therefore it works."

I needed to get some air.

The individual cars were divided by narrow, awning-covered platforms that shifted with the train as it bent along the track. As I crossed between the cars, I found a door leading to the outside. I expected it to be locked, but when I grabbed the handle the door slid to the side and opened to the rushing expanse of blackness outside the train.

My initial vertigo passed and I stared out at the darkest night I had ever seen. The light from the train illuminated the ground just beyond the tracks but faded quickly into a deep, empty void. Overhead the stars felt very close. I thought of the meteor shower in the cornfield. Now I was in India, on the other side of the world. The air was warm. I sat, legs dangling over the edge, and watched. I replayed the conversation with the Indian man over and over in my mind, hearing his story and feeling

his conviction and faltering in my certainty that he, rather than
I, was missing something. Here the idea of power and magic and
otherworldly forces did not seem far away at all. The border
between reality and fantasy felt very thin, as if the train could
accidentally cross over at any minute and arrive not in Varanasi
or even India but rather in Neverland or at the North Pole.

Here is knowledge. The rest is mystery. There is so much yet to be
discovered.

~

WHEN I RETURNED to my car, the daytime benches had been
converted to bunks and I climbed into the empty top berth.
I had been trying to start Thomas Merton's New Seeds of
Contemplation for the past few days and pulled out my flashlight
to read. The bunk was remarkably comfortable and the train
rocked gently on the tracks. It was very late. I was asleep before
I even opened the book, and the flashlight stayed on all night.

In the morning I woke to the sound of shouting. I pulled
aside the curtain and saw a man—a very loud man—wearing a
large vacuum-cleaner-shaped metal samovar on a strap across
his back. He bellowed the words "chai wallah" over and over
while dispensing tea through a hose into small terracotta cups
for five rupees apiece. I ordered one.

The tea was very hot and smelled delicious. I climbed down
from the bunk and carried my cup of tea back between the cars
and opened the door to the world from last night so I could sit
and drink and watch India roll by.

Outside the sky was bright, and the landscape—a rural stretch
of fields lined with telephone poles and short scrub trees—
looked so much like Iowa that if I had taken a picture and sent

it home no one would have believed that it came from the other side of the world. A man walked with a small herd of goats across one of the fields. The occasional cow looked up as we passed but most of them ignored us. A cell phone tower stood on the horizon. I heard someone announce "Varanasi" from inside the car, and the outskirts of a town came into view a few miles ahead.

I returned to my bunk for my bag and decided that my current shirt could survive another day. I could wash it that night at the hostel. I had a little water left in my bottle and used it to brush my teeth and wipe my face. Andy appeared with his bag already packed, and as the train slowed into the station everyone shuffled to the door. I turned around and saw the family from the night before. The son was attempting to read and walk down the aisle at the same time and the mom helped the daughter with her bag. The man waved and approached.

"Good morning, Magician." He seemed glad to see me. "Have you thought about our conversation from last night?"

I said that I had.

"I want you to remember what I said about tricks. This is the most important thing. You cannot call a thing fake unless you know the real, and you can't call a thing real unless you know the fake. I have seen the real. I know it exists. There are people here who have power. And if you spend some time in India, you may find them."

His wife caught his attention and he raised his hand in farewell, but passengers moving in every direction crowded the platform so completely that for a moment forward progress was impossible and the man and I stood trapped together in that awkward silence that comes after saying goodbye and then discovering it's impossible to leave. It couldn't have been later than eight or nine in the morning but the heat was already oppressive. Last night in the dark, as the train rushed through the fields and all I could see was the light from the windows and the vast, open canopy of stars, the world felt new and I felt new in it. Now all of that was gone. Here in the heat and the crush of people departing the train I couldn't focus beyond my immediate surroundings.

A gap finally opened in the crowd of travelers and the man followed his family into it, nodding and bobbing in farewell and then vanishing forever. Andy and I ascended the main staircase into the station. At the other end of the room I saw an archway, and beyond, a mass of people, rickshaws, taxis, and noise. The noise was incredible—honking, shouting, bartering, engines firing, dogs barking, mothers calling to children, taxi drivers hustling for business. And the smell—the smell hit me right away: people, livestock, burning gasoline, dark exhaust. The vehicles had kicked up dust in the air that blew in through the archway, welcoming us to the city. My first impression of Varanasi was absolute chaos, and I tried to embrace it.

THE SNAKE CHARMER

TIME WAS DIFFERENT here. On tour I was accustomed to rolling out of bed, already on the move, and immediately breaking the day down into a series of next steps, action items, bullet points on a list, crossing them off as I went. So far I hadn't been able to shake my habit of early rising—I suppose this had something to do with the time zone, too—but I'd lie still in my room and listen to the wind coming up the river, or head out into the courtyard when the world was still dark and sit facing east, waiting for the sun to rise over the opposite shore. I could think, not about work but about the ideas behind the work, or maybe I'd just sit and not think, and this was a revelation. I had been working like a madman for years—when I found Houdini's quote about working from seven A.M. to midnight I took him seriously. For some kids it's football. For others it's grades. For me it was always practice, and for the first time in years I didn't feel busy yet didn't feel as if I was wasting time, either. On tour I had been chasing something from venue to venue, room to room, moving across the country, and it had led me here. So I was here, and for the moment I was happy to figure the rest out as I went.

A few days after arriving in Varanasi I woke just before sunrise and walked down the stairs through the open-air court-yard. I sat on a chair at the edge of the patio overlooking the Ganges, thinking about tea and something to eat and waiting for the restaurant to open. The air was already warm. The sky was pink and yellow. Below I could see a solitary flute player at the edge of the water, and the sound of his music joined the slap of wet clothes on stone as men did laundry by the banks of the river. A pack of monkeys ran the roofline of a building and disap-peared into a tree. By midday the color on these buildings would look sun-worn and faded, but the early-morning light made them glow and the entire city shimmered—red, blue, yellow. On a balcony across from me a father carried a tray of teacups and a mother ushered her children to sit and drink. A goat wandered haphazardly down the long staircase to the river. Every road in the city leads eventually to the river. It's the center of everything.

As I watched the city begin its day I noticed Andy a hundred yards down, camera in hand. I didn't know he was already up. Apparently he got what he wanted with the camera and began the long climb up the staircase to our hotel.

"Is the restaurant open yet?" He sat down across from me.

"Almost, I think. I heard them in there a minute ago."

"I wanted to get some good shots of the sunrise before we head over there." He looked up and smiled. "Are you ready?"

"Not before breakfast I'm not," I said. "He won't be there yet anyway."

"They said nine, so you have some time." Andy was enjoying this too much. "But," he added, "you don't want to keep him waiting."

"I know they said nine," I said. "I haven't been able to think about anything else."

Yesterday I had done magic for a group of kids at an open plaza by the river and learned that the snake charmer came there most days around nine in the morning. *Surely he will be there tomorrow*, they said. *You should come. We will meet you there and help you speak with him. Ha-ha! It is settled. We will see you then.*

I don't want to dwell on this, but I'm a terrible coward when it comes to snakes. Even snakes on TV make me pick my feet up off the ground and sit cross-legged on the couch. I came to India to see traditional Indian magic, and I knew from the beginning that this would include snake charmers, but it didn't really occur to me that this would mean coming so close to the snakes, too. Not just pictures of snakes. Real snakes. Cobras.

All of this was on my mind as we walked along the river to the plaza a few minutes later. From water level Varanasi looked incomprehensible. Buildings had been stacked between and piled on top of other buildings, rising up from the riverbank to form an uneven wall of balconies, balustrades, plazas, and overlooks, all bound together by a great labyrinth of twisting staircases and narrow streets no wider than sidewalks. Andy had his camera out as we approached the plaza and I concentrated on acting brave in case his footage ever turned into anything that other people might watch. The street children from yesterday were there, and by the looks of things many had brought their parents or older siblings who no doubt came to watch the silly American magician who is afraid of snakes. One of the children pretended to slither over toward me, hissing. I did not like this at all.

The snake charmer sat in a corner of the plaza. He wore a gray beard and ancient sandals and struck me as someone who had crossed vast distances on foot. He sat back on his heels and held a long, double-barreled flute with both hands. Before him, two large lidded baskets rested on the ground, waiting.

I crouched in front of him and raised a hand to say hello. He bowed his head and looked up, evaluating, I think, but kindly. When he finally spoke, one of the kids began to translate.

"You are the magician?"

I nodded. He thought about this for a moment, then raised the flute to his mouth and began to play.

The sound was thin and jangly—a hypnotic, pentatonic melody that raised the hair on the back of my neck. He looped it over and over, two melodies trading places and then weaving together to create a third. The music was shrill and haunting, part warning, part enchantment, and it put me on edge. Somehow it sounded like both a car alarm and a lullaby.

Deliberately, carefully, the snake charmer took one hand from the flute and lifted the lid from each basket. At first, nothing. He continued to play. The baskets sat, open and dreadful, and I stared, waiting. Then, with the unhurried confidence possessed only by the truly powerful, the cobras rose up to take stock of their surroundings.

They were enormous—two cobras each as thick as my arm, uncoiling themselves impossibly high until they stood two feet in the air, their heavy heads swaying almost imperceptibly to the music, like sunflowers in a failing breeze. One flicked her tongue and then slowly, deliberately turned her gaze in my direction. She saw me.

I was transfixed with fear.

Fear, I think, is very close to wonder. Even then as I tried to keep my composure I was aware in some distant corner of my consciousness that this was one of the most amazing experiences I'd ever had. I thought back to the reactions I've seen at some of my performances—people jumping back, running away, shouting "No! No! No!" over and over. At that moment I knew how they felt.

For years I had wondered if the powerful reactions to even simple magic tricks could be explained by humanity's fear of death. I wondered, for instance, if the teacher on the playground had responded with such force because—having just seen what looked like a miracle—she was forced to reconsider the possibility of all miracles, including the possibility that death is only provisional. This theory disintegrated for me the first time I performed magic for young children. When I was just out of college a preschool nearby asked if I could come in to do magic for the kids. There, three- and four-year-old children who were far too young to have any sense of their own mortality responded with the same wild, tremulous joy as the adults.

My next theory was that a magician is tapping into humanity's inherent fear of the unknown. We like order and structure. Even when we tell ourselves otherwise, we like a domesticated worldview that fits comfortably within the limits of our own knowledge and understanding. Usually a magic trick doesn't threaten this at all. We see it as a trick and know it is a trick, and we are comfortable with things that we can classify as tricks. But once in a while—when the magic is so good that it doesn't feel like a trick but instead feels *real*—then the carefully ordered story that we tell ourselves about our understanding of the universe is overturned and upset. *I don't believe in magic, but I have just seen magic.* The result is fear, and joy, in varying degrees according to the individual, but any mixture of the two is almost indistinguishable from wonder.

In the face of the cobra I had another idea. Wonder and fear are similar in the way they both temporarily defeat the ego and allow you the extraordinary experience of seeing the world outside the confines of your own identity. Every day we wake up and choose the clothes we wear, the words we say, the actions we take, and the demeanor we carry at least in part as an effort to communicate something about ourselves to the rest of the world. There's a kind of performance that goes on when you choose the Ramones T-shirt instead of the polo or the thick-rimmed glasses instead of the contact lenses—we want the world to consider us in a certain light, and we go to great lengths to make this happen. A moment of genuine astonishment or fear makes this all fall away. You are not concerned with your identity, desires, or motivations. You just exist, a part of everything. When the cobra looked at me I wasn't thinking about myself or the way I was perceived by others. All of that was gone. For a moment everything was simple and clear. I was awake and alive. The snake's tongue flitted out, tasting the air, and she fanned her hood wide. Our eyes met.

I was in awe of this creature.

I had read as much as I could about snake charming before coming to India but none of it had prepared me for the eye contact. You couldn't capture it in any photograph. She stared at me, personally, directly, and in that moment I discovered the primal and hopeless fear that comes from the open, welcoming gaze of a cobra who knows you are within striking distance. It turned me liquid and powerless. I understood immediately why the cobra is holy in this part of the world—an angel of death, maybe, but an angel for certain. Her head moved so slightly from one side to the other, rocking gently, gracefully, and if you were mystically inclined you might feel she was hypnotizing you before the fatal bite to ease your passage from the world of the living to the world of the dead. This cobra did not look charmed or domesticated. She looked wild and fierce, and wide, wide awake.

At this point I was maybe four feet from the baskets. I had been even closer but retreated—scooted—backward when the cobras appeared. This delighted the peanut gallery, who kept up a running commentary consisting mostly of laughter and the occasional English phrase such as "He is very scared!" and "Look! Look! He jumps!" Annoyance, along with an unsteady resolve to see this through to the end, was enough to start me forward again to get as close as I could.

The Internet is full of theories about snake charming, and as I crawled forward I ran through as many as I could remember. First, apparently snakes don't have ears, so the music must be more for me than for the snakes. What keeps the snakes upright? The prevailing theory is that the snakes are afraid of the tip of the flute and sway back and forth to keep it in sight. The snake charmer did keep the end of his flute in constant motion, but I noticed that neither of the cobras paid any attention to him. One stared out at the crowd, unfazed. The other was still looking directly at me.

The allegation of animal abuse prompted the Indian government to pass the Wildlife Protection Act in 1972, effectively outlawing the practice of snake charming by making it illegal to domesticate a wild animal. Though the law covers a much broader list of species, in part this legislation came as a response to the growing outcry against snake charmers who were thought to break the fangs off their snakes and cauterize their poison glands to eradicate the danger. Some apparently went so far as to sew the mouths of the cobras shut and drug them into lethargy. This sounded bad when I read about it, but there in front of that majestic animal it felt like an unpardonable crime. These snakes didn't look drugged, but I needed to get closer if I was going to see their fangs.

I moved to the side of the basket and began my approach, crawling carefully forward at the rate of about one foot a minute. One of the cobras continued to look out at the world— passive, content, uninterested. The other kept an eye on me. I was on all fours now, crouching low, trying to look brave but fooling no one. The spectators kept talking and one of the children lunged forward, clapping his hands together to frighten the snake, who reared back and up, impossibly high, fanning her hood out wide. She arched her back and hissed—defensive and hostile, putting us all on notice. She looked magnificent. I wanted her to slip out of the basket and flee to the river, but she lowered herself back down and resumed her death stare in my direction as if all of this was my fault.

We were both on edge now—the snake and I—and when I started to move forward again she decided she had put up with us for long enough. I watched, frozen and unbelieving, as she spilled over the side of her basket, fluid and unstoppable, like water through a broken dam. She lifted her head from the ground and towered before us, hissing and flashing her eyes, and then dropped to the ground and spun her coils in a smooth, muscular, endless arc. She turned away from the crowd and darted toward the river.

Unfortunately, this set me directly in her path, and I quickly lost all interest in theories about snake charming and any desire to see her fangs. I was the only thing between her life in the basket and the freedom of the river, and she shot forward. I fell backward over myself and shouted *"Holy goddamned mother-fucking shit!"* as I tripped out of the way. Then I ran. When I turned back after fifteen or twenty feet I saw the snake dangling by the tail as the snake charmer gently fed her back into her wicker basket. He spoke to her softly, saying "It's okay, it's okay." I wondered how close to me she had actually come.

The peanut gallery thought this was the funniest thing they had ever seen. They pointed at me and laughed. "He hops! He hops!" "Look! Look! He runs away! He is afraid!"

This was not going well.

The snake charmer placed the lids back on the baskets and motioned for me to sit next to him. We spoke about my trip and his life with the cobras. Apparently the snake charming act was just a side job. His main role was as a snake catcher who removes cobras from populated areas and releases them into the wild. He caught his two current cobras in Haridwar—a town near the northern border of India. We spoke about the cobra and how he saw his work as an act of devotion to this holy animal.

"You are very afraid?"

I nodded.

He thought about this for a moment. Then he asked me to stand. He went to the basket and lifted the lid. When the cobra stuck her head out to look around, he gently grasped her behind the head and supported her weight with his other hand as she slid out of the basket.

"I will hold her head," he said, and indicated that I should lift my arms. He stood next to me and placed the cobra in my hands. She felt like one continuous muscle, like she could strike through a wall if she wanted. She was at least six feet long, probably seven, and her dry, black scales felt smooth and hard, like small stones. I was astonished by her weight.

The sun had climbed high enough for the heat to feel unbearable. I was hot, the cobra was hot, and neither of us was taking this particularly well. I think the cobra could feel my anxiety. She twitched and I heard a squirt and suddenly my hands were covered in cobra shit, yellow and thin. The snake sprang forward into the arms of the snake charmer and I jumped away, hollering. The snake charmer put the cobra back into the basket, taking his time about it. I sat on the steps, shocked, looking down at my hands.

Andy had been filming this entire encounter, and as he came over I had a terrible thought.

"Andy, is cobra shit poisonous?" I asked him.

"What?" He looked up from the camera.

"Is cobra shit *poisonous!*" I was now worried about the neurotoxic death shit all over my hands, and Andy is the sort of person you just assume would know this sort of thing.

One of the bystanders came over. "No no. Cobra shit is not poison."

~

An hour later we had installed ourselves outside a tea stand and were waiting for our second cup. The power of the tea stand to impose calm and comfort on this street was impressive, crowded as it was by a few dozen cars, maybe a hundred rickshaws, two camels, a few dozen motorcycles, hundreds of pedestrians, a cow, a bus, and an oversized delivery truck, all honking, shouting, or bleating according to their nature and competing for the right of way. The din from the road was overpowering, and yet just a few feet from the curb we sheltered on the other side of the stand and somehow the cloves and cardamom from the tea cut through the smell of dust and burning diesel and made you feel that you could take a rest from the city for a minute.

The man in the tea stand had clearly spent years honing his craft and had elevated this beverage almost to the level of a sacrament. I admired the workmanlike way he handled his kit—no fuss, no latticework latte art with the foam on top. He just stood there all day in the heat and the noise and knocked out cup after cup of perfect tea. After the excitement of the morning this felt like a kind of miracle.

Andy had fallen into conversation with him and I sat on a plastic stool that used to be white and looked down at my feet in the dust of the road. I was thinking about the snake charmer—the snake catcher—and trying to imagine a situation in America when someone would cry "Quick, find the magician!" during a crisis. Other than entertainment, I wondered what real, tangible value someone in my profession could actually contribute to society. I know that some of the top card guys in magic moonlight as security consultants for casinos around the world, and sometimes a film production team will hire a magician to make a stunt look more impossible or a con more believable, but this seems unimportant compared to the snake charmer who plunges his bare hands into the sewers and basement corners of India to keep people safe from cobras.

I was thinking about some of my best shows and wondering how long that moment of wonder stayed with the audience. An hour? A day? And then it passes and I go on to do another show somewhere else, but other than the fading memory of the impossible I'm not sure I ever really gave anybody anything. It's hard to say.

I finished the second cup of tea and tried to taste it as long as I could. When I looked up, I noticed a crowd of people gathered next to the tea stand. The snake charmer stood in the middle of this group, waving at me and holding one of those industrial PVC paint buckets covered with a lid.

"He is asking for the magician." One of the tea stand patrons started translating for the snake charmer.

I stood. Suspicion. Worry. Dread.

"He says you are very lucky." I looked at the translator. He clarified, "He says you are very lucky for him. You have brought him good fortune."

"What's in the bucket?" I asked.

"This is an auspicious day, he says. On the same day he met you, he has also caught another cobra and believes you brought him this good fortune."

The snake charmer had put the bucket down on the ground and was motioning for everyone to stand back.

"You mean in the last hour he caught *another* cobra? Here? In Varanasi?"

"Yes," the translator said, "in the toilet of a house not far from here."

I had that feeling you get in horror movies when the camera moves in close and you know some evil creature lurks just out of the frame.

"Where was the house? What do you mean 'Not far from here'?"

But the snake charmer was talking again and the translator plowed ahead to keep up.

"He says he wishes to show you his new cobra to thank you for this good fortune. Watch."

My brain hadn't really moved on from the thought that other cobras were coiled in the pipes and toilets of this city, but events were moving on without me. The snake charmer had cleared a circle around the bucket and was working on the lid. Andy was up with the camera. I stood there, incredulous, watching.

A sound came from inside the bucket and then he got the lid off and we heard the sound again—a deep-throated hiss, and then another. This was the only warning we got. Faster than anything, a cobra rose from the bucket, up like a rocket as high as she could go. She was smaller than the others but made up for it with fury, flashing her eyes and hissing, her fangs clearly visible, her head darting, assessing escape routes, looking for options, or justice, or revenge. Again, I was simultaneously in awe of her magnificence and numb with fear. The group watched, dumb-struck, and Andy shouted "Shut her in the bucket! Shut her in the bucket!" She dropped her head, ready to dart into the crowd, but the snake charmer pushed her back inside with the lid and held it tightly to the top of the bucket. We heard the hissing again and the bucket shook as she roiled inside.

The snake charmer looked at me and we faced each other. He bowed. I bowed back.

~

THAT AFTERNOON ANDY and I sat at a table at the terrace restaurant of our hotel. The sun felt closer than usual. Everything—the air, the walls, the ground through my shoes, the glass tabletop, the plastic chair—everything was hot. I went to my room to wash my hands, which still carried the tang of yellow cobra shit, and returned to find Andy studying the menu, frowning.

"I'd like a beer," he said. "You?"

Never in my entire life had this sounded better.

The waiter came over. He was in his late teens, I think, and wore a brown cotton shirt under a crisp white apron. "Sir?"

"Hello," Andy began. "Could we please order two large Kingfishers?"

The waiter stepped back, bowing slightly and frowning apologetically. With genuine regret, he explained that local law prohibited the sale of alcohol during the day. Would we like tea instead?

Now, I will say this about Andy. He is magnificent under pressure. "This tea," he began, without missing a beat, "does it come in a teapot?"

"Sir?"

"Does it come in an enclosed pot?" He formed a teapot with his hands to demonstrate.

"Yes, sir." The waiter looked at Andy carefully.

"And the cups—are they ceramic? Opaque?"

"Yes, sir. Ceramic cups, for tea."

"Okay, sorry to ask so many questions," Andy said, "I just want to clarify. If the tea comes in a ceramic pot and we drink the tea out of teacups, isn't it true that no one could see the color of the tea we are drinking?"

The waiter began to smile and we were now part of a conspiracy. "Sir, it is a very old law. If someone saw us serving alcohol we would be punished. But if they didn't see us, we would not be punished, and I should add that I have no personal objection to the serving of alcohol during the day."

"In that case, would it be possible to order two large pots of this *special tea?*" Andy said, indicating Kingfisher beer on the menu.

The waiter grinned, sealing our cabal. "Absolutely, sir. Two large pots of special tea it is."

He disappeared into the kitchen and we heard him say something to someone, followed by laughter. A head poked out of the doorway, looked in our direction, and returned to the kitchen. More laughter. Apparently we were a riot. Two minutes later our waiter reappeared, flanked by two additional staff. Everyone was grinning. They carried two teapots. Andy thanked them profusely.

The tea was wonderful.

GODMEN

I DIDN'T KNOW THEIR names. I don't think they ever knew mine either. To them, I was simply the magician who had traveled from America and now spent every morning hanging out by the river. To me, they were a disorganized gang of fifteen to twenty kids that roamed the neighborhoods of Varanasi and liked to see magic. In return, they helped me on my search. *Want to meet a snake charmer? Meet us here tomorrow at nine. You want to meet a holy man? We call them* sadhus—*right this way. Now you have to teach us a trick. My father has a tea stand and if you do magic for the customers I bet he will give you some tea. Come this way and I will show you.*

These kids and their families became my de facto ambassadors to the side of the city that most tourists never get to see. Their parents—as interested as the children as to why an American magician would come to Varanasi—shared meals, tea, advice, knowledge. They invited me to the neighborhood pickup cricket game, asked me to do magic for their relatives and friends, and allowed me to insinuate myself—however briefly—into the day-to-day life of this city that would have been otherwise inaccessible.

One morning I was doing magic for them by the river when a man approached.

He looked like a pirate, or a wizard. He stood directly in front of me, wrapped in a complicated array of orange and yellow cloth trimmed in places with gold plastic ribbon and held together by strips of what appeared to be a torn white bedsheet. He stepped through the crowd to the front and interrupted by raising his hand toward me, saying "Yes yes yes yes yes yes yes yes yes."

"Hi, okay," I said.

"Yes yes yes yes yes yes," he said again. He was thin and tall. Around his waist, a golden braided rope held a silver pitcher and an empty paint can that rattled when he moved. He carried a wicker bedroll under one arm and wore a kind of cloth crown on top of his head.

A sadhu, I thought. Varanasi was famous for its holy men— known as sadhus—who spend their lives in ascetic devotion to various strands of Hinduism. The day before, I had met another sadhu by the river, but other than repeating the words "all is one, all is one" over and over, he didn't want to talk.

I was interested in the sadhus for a few reasons, the first being that I'm fascinated by those who devote their lives to one pursuit to the exclusion of all else. Houdini pretended to live like a superstar, but he worked seventeen hours out of every twenty-four, never smoked, never drank, exercised constantly, and completely gave himself over to his craft. This isn't the same thing as a life of hermetic meditation, certainly, but the two are more similar to each other than they are to the common life of work and leisure. So I wanted to talk to a sadhu about his existence and learn more about the practicalities of a life of devotion.

Also, a particular type of sadhu—the *aghori*—are said to practice black magic. I didn't know what that meant, and I wanted to learn more.

All of this ran through my mind as the sadhu stood before me. He began to speak, and one of the spectators translated for me. " 'Practice makes perfect,' he is saying. 'You practice and that is how you can do your magic.' He says if he practiced, he could do also."

"Once again," the sadhu said, pointing back and forth between us. "Once again." He wanted to see magic.

He sat in front of me, requiring a full minute to settle in comfortably, like a cat circling tediously before finally sitting down. He repeatedly rearranged the various folds and twists of his garment, unaided in this by the paint can and silver pitcher, which kept sliding along the rope into his lap. Once he had completed these adjustments to his satisfaction he looked at me impatiently and indicated that I should get on with it. I stared at him, bemused, and then showed him a simple piece of sleight of hand—I burned a match, then held it closed in my fist, and when I opened my hand the match was unburned. One of the parents shouted once and then began to clap. Others laughed. But the sadhu didn't respond at all. He just stared at me, unblinking, and I thought of the cobra in the bucket. He said something I couldn't understand.

"He wants to talk to you," the spectator said. The others were shuffling their feet and looking around. A few wandered off. The sadhu raised his hand for silence and then began, in English.

"Your god, my god. Your god, my god. Yes yes yes yes yes yes yes."

I looked at him.

"Your god, my god. Yes. Your god, my god. Yes yes yes yes yes yes."

These appeared to be the only English words he knew, but he made the most of them. This wasn't the conversation I had hoped for. I heard two of the children laughing. "They laugh because you are listening so earnestly to a madman," the translator explained, imitating me and furrowing his eyebrows in concentration. "He is just crazy. What he says is nothing."

"Good night, good morning," the sadhu was saying now. "Good night, good morning. Good night, good morning."

"Isn't he a holy man?" I asked one of the spectators. "A sadhu?"

Everyone laughed. "No holy man. No sadhu. He is a freeman—he just travels from place to place asking for money. See?"

The freeman held his paint can toward me. "Yes yes yes yes yes."

The whole group was still laughing at me when a large man wearing a Styrofoam tray walked into the midst of our huddle and asked if we wanted to buy any Popsicles. "Ice cream? Ice cream?"

The freeman immediately raised his hand and the ice cream seller handed him a yellow Popsicle.

"Money, money?" the vendor asked. The freeman pointed to me.

"Money," the vendor demanded, this time talking to me.

"How much?" I asked.

"Five rupees."

I pulled out a note.

"No!" shouted a young boy who had been watching the magic—noble soul, he—"One rupee only. Five is too many!"

I paid for the Popsicle and made the change disappear. The ice cream merchant looked at me strangely and hurried away.

~

WORD SPREAD. An American magician was in Varanasi and he could do amazing things. I wasn't famous, of course, but we were the only Americans we saw in that part of the city and Andy brought the camera everywhere, so we were conspicuous. Sometimes the crowds got uncomfortably large. Andy had obtained permits to film in Varanasi but I certainly didn't have permission to give performances. I hadn't come here to perform, but I had learned that it opened doors that might have been closed otherwise. Unfortunately, the police were notoriously strict about street performing. When I did magic, Andy would keep a lookout, and we worked out a signal—a rapid tugging on his earlobe—to let me know if the police were coming.

One morning I was doing magic for a group of rickshaw drivers. One of them was about to turn over the top card of the deck and find the ace of spades, and it was going to feel like a miracle.

"What's your name?" I asked.

"Dabbu," he responded, not taking his eyes from the top of the deck.

"Dabbu," I said, "turn over the top card." He did, and immediately I realized we had a problem. The group—which had grown considerably since I began doing magic five minutes ago, now extended well out into the street, and while a moment ago they were quietly straining for a better view, now they were all reacting to the illusion and this looked uncomfortably like a riot. Dabbu raised his hands and covered his eyes. The man next to him slapped him on the shoulder. Everyone was shouting. "Nate," Andy said, but it was hard to hear him and I was trying to bring the group back down. I raised my hands and tried to speak but everyone was too loud. "Nate!" Andy said again, and this time I looked over to see what he wanted. He was pulling on his earlobe.

"Do you have your rickshaw nearby?" I asked Dabbu. He nodded. "Good. Can you get us out of here?"

Andy was already hauling me through the crowd by the loop on my backpack and Dabbu steered us to his rickshaw on the edge of the street. I was astonished at how large the group had grown. A row of men sat on a low wall for a better view and the spectators had spilled out onto the road, blocking the traffic. Dabbu's rickshaw was green and yellow and Andy and I slid onto the back bench as he started the engine. "Where are you going?" he asked.

"Anywhere," Andy shouted. "Just go!"

A rickshaw ride is harrowing even under normal circumstances, but Dabbu grasped the urgency of the situation and we hurtled down the narrow street, horn blaring, as cows, cyclists, and pedestrians hurried to clear the way. He leaned over the handlebars, throttle wide open, and this was maybe the first time in my life I have ever needed to make a real getaway. We emerged onto a main street and blended into the cars, trucks, and dozens of other yellow and green rickshaws.

I leaned back in the seat and watched as we rushed toward two carts, separated by a very small space, and we passed between them at full speed with only inches on either side. The air was filled with dust from the road and the incessant honking to say "Watch out!" and "I am here!" and "There you are!" and "We are going!" Dabbu honked—good long blares of the horn—at least once every five or ten seconds whether or not we were near anyone, which appeared to be the standard practice for every vehicle on the road.

"How long are you being in Varanasi?" Dabbu asked once we were in the relative calm of this major thoroughfare.

"Another day or so," I said. "We don't really have a plan."

"One day more you stay in Varanasi," Dabbu said, as if thinking to himself of all that could possibly be fit into one day in this city.

"How many years are you?" he asked.

"Twenty-six," I replied. "How old are you?"

"I am thirty-one," he said.

"Are you married?"

"I am married," he said, and when I asked if he had children he replied "Two boys," but I heard it as "Two wives!" and asked him about it.

"No! No! One wife. One wife! Muslim families may have many wives, but in Hindu families, just one wife. Two b-o-y-s! One eight years old and one three years old." He spent a moment chuckling to himself about the absurdity of having two wives, apparently gleeful at having escaped such a predicament.

He asked about my family.

"Yes, I am married."

"Is your wife here in Varanasi?"

"No. No, she's in Iowa."

Dabbu was silent for a moment as he drove.

"Iowa is very far?" he asked.

"Yes. Iowa is very far."

THOUGH I DIDN'T know it at the time, not everyone who saw my performance that morning appreciated the magic. That afternoon a man approached me near a tea stand and pointed his finger at my chest.

"Earlier I saw you doing the things," he said, moving his hands like he was performing a magic trick, "and I said to myself, 'I do not want to watch that man. I know he is a deceiver.'"

While on tour in the United States I have been protested, heckled, booed, dismissed, ignored, and insulted—sometimes all in the same show—but this man appeared to dislike me more than anyone else I had ever met. He was smiling—in fact, he was all smiles, but it was a mocking, derisive sort of smile, like you find at the sort of parties where everyone is trying to be cleverer than everyone else. He was slightly shorter than me, and rail thin, and he spoke with the unshakable certainty I had come to associate with both religious fundamentalists and hard-line atheists, or anyone who considers their beliefs the only possible truth. I didn't know how to respond.

"Other people were eager to come and see you," he continued, "but I was sitting right here and I did not come. I said to myself, 'He is using tricks. He knows nothing about what is magic. In fact, he knows nothing.'" He smiled.

I thought this was taking it a little far and I asked him how he knew I wasn't using actual supernatural powers to accomplish my magic—an obnoxious question, certainly, but he had riled me.

"We have a saying in my tradition. 'The more a man knows, the more he remains silent.' If you had supernatural power, you would also have the sense not to show it around on the street corner like a common beggar. Because you are showing it around on the street corner, I am confident you do not have supernatural power. You are using tricks. And I should tell you that not everyone knows you are using tricks. You should be careful of spreading superstition so carelessly."

He was not smiling now.

A few years earlier while on tour in the States I noticed a woman leaving the show early, visibly upset, and an hour later on my way out to the car I found her waiting for me by the theater door. She was convinced I had enlisted the aid of demonic spirits to accomplish the magic and wanted to warn me of the danger.

"I was uncomfortable during your show," she said, "because I felt spiritual energy all around you as you did those things onstage. I could hear the voices whispering to you during your show. I could hear them tell you everything you needed to perform that magic."

At first I'd thought she was angry, but her voice quavered during this speech and I realized it wasn't anger. It was fear, and suddenly I was grateful that I couldn't see the vision of the universe confronting her at that moment.

"I want you to know that what you're doing is incredibly dangerous. You are opening yourself up to an awful power that I don't think you understand."

I tried to explain that I was using magic tricks to create the experience of magic and that while I wanted the pieces in the show to feel real in the moment, they weren't real. They were illusions. "Do you want me to explain how it worked?" I offered.

"No, those powers are very real," she said before turning to leave. "You have to be very careful."

In the world of professional magic a great debate surrounds the practice of offering a disclaimer at the beginning of a show— something like *"In the next hour you may come to believe that I have supernatural powers. I do not, and I want to be clear that I do not. I'm using a set of secret skills and techniques to create the illusion of magic, but none of this is real. Now, on with the show."* Some see this as unnecessary and even unhelpful. Imagine how completely it would ruin the atmosphere if a film director appeared at the beginning of a movie to say "Remember folks, all of this is fake." But many, many practitioners in my business do this at the beginning of every performance. Partly it's an artistic choice. If you assume that a modern, intelligent audience will naturally suspect that everything in a magic show is fake, telling them that it's fake at the beginning of the show and then amazing them anyway forces them to confront the difference between their intellectual understanding and their emotional experience.

When you're amazed by something, part of that experience is the rapid realization that your previous understanding of existence was too limited to accommodate this new thing you've just seen. This could be as mild as witnessing a display of extraordinary skill—say, a YouTube video of a mountain biker racing down an implausibly narrow ridge, deftly maneuvering the bike over the trail with thousand-foot sheer drops inches away on either side—and having to suddenly expand your assumptions about human bravery and physical ability. It could be as large as looking up into the depths of the Milky Way one night and realizing with awe and regret that somewhere along the way your working awareness of the universe had shrunk to fit the parameters of your everyday life, that you had inflated the importance of small concerns and ignored your connection to the wider world around you. Big or small, these jolts of expanding awareness are a fundamental component of the experience of wonder. Magic tricks are very good at facilitating these moments.

But there's also an ethical consideration. If your view of reality already allows for the possibility of vanishing coins, or thoughts traveling from one mind to another by magic, or demonic spirits helping the magician to perform miracles, then a magic trick doesn't expand your view of reality but instead just reinforces it. If you believe in ghosts, and I do a magic trick where you actually feel that you have seen a ghost, I'm not amazing you so much as confirming what you already believe. You might be surprised—surely most people who believe in ghosts have never actually seen one—but I'm really just giving you evidence in support of your convictions. If I don't share your convictions or am in a position to benefit from them whether or not they're true, suddenly I'm treading on pretty thin ethical ice. A magic trick that feels real and forces you to consider the boundaries of your own certainty is a good thing. But if I convince you to believe a magic trick is real and then encourage you to come to me for spiritual guidance, the ice melts entirely. In India, this is a big problem.

Indian "Godmen" pose as spiritual leaders, or gurus, and deceive their followers by presenting ordinary, run-of-the-mill sleight-of-hand magic tricks as actual, supernatural miracles. They are the televangelists of India—the snake-oil salesmen, the revivalist preachers with a hidden Tesla coil, promising a 9-volt surge of God's own healing power for the price of a ten-dollar ticket and a donation to the ministry, credit cards accepted. A recent article in the *India Times* featured seven Godmen who are now in prison for extorting vast sums of money from their followers, but their exploitation doesn't end with money. Of the seven, four are also imprisoned for multiple counts of rape, two for the murder of an outspoken critic, and one for running a prostitution ring out of his spiritual learning center. They use magic tricks to establish themselves as miraculous emis-saries of the gods on earth—divinely inspired, exempt from the laws and moral codes of the merely mortal.

Magic—with its ability to deceive even the clever and analytical people in a Godman's following of thousands—is the perfect tool. Want to levitate in front of your followers? No problem. You can buy the equipment for a rudimentary levitation illusion for about nine hundred dollars. Want to read someone's mind? Again, no problem. There are hundreds of books that can teach you how to do that, or at least how to fake it.

Spiritual deception is not just an Indian problem. It happens everywhere, and it has throughout history. In the collection of magic books I discovered at the Ames Public Library as a young boy, I remember a chapter on the history of magic featuring schematic drawings of an ancient Greek temple, equipped with primitive smoke machines and stage effects intended to simulate a divine presence, all triggered by a catch on the temple door. The Greek peasant would mount the steps, open the door, and—*cue the smoke, cue the fire, cue the gong*—encounter the presence of

Zeus, right there on a Thursday morning. From the snake-handling churches of modern America to the false mystics in Nepal who utilize a standard, off-the-shelf levitation illusion available from magic stores worldwide to convince the gullible of their spiritual power, the history of religion is blighted by those who present magic tricks as divinely ordained, supernatural miracles in an effort to elevate their own status.

But the practice of using traditional sleight-of-hand-style deception to simulate spiritual power has been perfected to the highest possible degree by the modern Indian Godman. The decentralized nature of Hinduism—which has no papacy or other political governing body that might be able to clamp down on this kind of criminality—and the extraordinary sophistication of the modern magician's technique have created a perfect environment for the unscrupulous guru. The Godman walks into a village—out in the country, maybe, where most of the people are uneducated and less likely to cause trouble—and performs a few miracles. Maybe he secretly sprinkles some potassium permanganate under a few sticks and then blesses them with water—actually glycerine—and they burst into flame. Maybe he walks across a bed of hot coals, or stabs a skewer through his arm without bleeding, or spits fire from his mouth like a dragon. People talk. Word gets around. And when the time comes to ask for a donation, the Godman has already proved himself worthy. Just look at the miracles. He collects their tribute, welcomes them into his following, and moves on.

So if you're an aspiring millionaire and have no misgivings about criminal fraud, becoming a Godman can be a profitable business move. The overhead is cheap—all you need is a few simple magic tricks—and you can just make up the spiritual message as you go. One of the imprisoned Godmen still maintains a website—complete with a fully functional online donation system—replete with kernels of his towering spiritual insight such as "We were born to be helpful to others."

When I was a child learning about magic, I discovered that Houdini had dedicated the last years of his life to a campaign against a similar phenomenon in America. In the 1920s, hordes of fraudulent mediums used magic techniques to simulate contact with the dead. For a fee, these charlatan psychics would hold a séance and help you communicate with a loved one or a friend who had passed away, and in these years immediately following World War I, speaking with the dead became a very profitable business.

Houdini's strategy was brilliant. Each night he packed the theaters and performed his own grand illusions as promised, but he devoted the third act of each show to the exposure of these fraudulent practices. First he would demonstrate a séance and ghosts would dance, invisible bells would ring, messages from the great beyond would appear—and then he would turn on the lights and show everyone how it all worked.

Today, the magicians of India have launched a similar campaign against the Godmen. Through a partnership with the Indian Rationalist Association they've created a series of educational lectures intended to expose these false prophets and explain how their miracles are actually just clever decep-tions. First the lecturer enters the village disguised as a Godman, performs the miracles, and attracts as many followers as possible.

Then he pulls back the proverbial curtain and teaches everyone the trick.

~

THE MAN OUTSIDE the tea stand reprimanded me for spreading superstition for about fifteen minutes. He resented India's image in the wider world as a Land of Mystery and worried the country's mystical heritage overshadowed its accomplishments in the arts and sciences. Many people of the Western world are drawn to India's magical past—especially magicians—but conversations with locals made it clear that much of India is ready to shed this image of mysticism. "Everything has a scientific explanation," the man told me emphatically. "In India we believe in science."

He's right, of course. India has the seventh-largest and currently the fastest-growing economy in the world, boasts a number of world-class universities, and—less quantifiably but equally impressive—has largely succeeded in sustaining a population of 1.25 billion people in a part of the world frequently gripped by famine, drought, and shortage. None of this happened by accident or luck. India is chaotic, wild, and turbulent, certainly, but it is also a thriving nation on the path to prosperity. Again and again on my trip I encountered people who voiced the same sentiment: "We believe in science. Everything has a scientific explanation."

So why the reputation for mysticism and magic?

In Peter Lamont's *The Rise of the Indian Rope Trick*, he traces India's image as a land of wonder and mystery to the rise of British colonial rule in India and the orientalist—which is to say, racist—lens through which the early-nineteenth-century

West perceived the East: uneducated, uncivilized, and in need of a more refined culture to come in and take control. In short, it was in the interests of the ruling powers of the West to portray India as a superstitious backwater in order to justify their occupation and control of its people, government, and markets. But this perception served another need of the West as well. The Enlightenment and its accompanying waves of discovery and innovation had filled in most of the blank spots on the map by the end of the eighteenth century, and everyone likes blank spots on the map. Near the end of his book Lamont writes, "In a modern West that has dis-enchanted itself in the name of science and progress, a magical East was required to satisfy the deeper human need for wonder."

In other words, Westerners still want mystery but prefer to keep it safely on the other side of the world. We want our daily existence built on the solid rock of logic and reason, so we pick somewhere far away and say *There, that's where the magic lives—in India, the Land of Mystery.*

When I read about these ideas while on tour in America they felt straightforward and easy to understand, especially because as a magician I'd witnessed this same impulse on a smaller scale over and over again. Every night during my show I'd see people in the audience torn between their inherent love of the unknown and their desire to explain it all away—to take just as much strangeness as was comfortable and attempt to banish the rest.

But in India the issue felt more complicated. I thought of the man on the train to Varanasi who had first assured me that he believed solely in science and then proceeded to tell me about the time someone cast a spell on his sister using "superior mental strength." I was willing to believe that much of India's magical reputation had been created by the West—and certainly, belief in the magical and the supernatural can be found in every country and culture in the history of the world—but you couldn't escape the abundance of mysticism here. It was everywhere.

CHOOMANTAR

As ANDY AND I drove through Varanasi one night, squeezed into a rickshaw with a man we'd just met an hour before, I reflected that I had no idea where we were going. It's only an adventure if you're willing to get lost, I had reasoned fifteen minutes earlier, but as the rickshaw hurtled through the late-evening traffic and the hotel disappeared farther and farther behind us, I came to understand that at this particular moment I was very lost, and the romantic spirit of discovery that marks the beginning of trips like this had given way to the doubt and uncertainty found so easily in the middle.

Two days earlier, while seeking permits for Andy to film by the river, we'd met a film producer named Rashmi—a high Brahman aristocrat with a full white beard. When he learned I was traveling across India to search for magic he offered to arrange a meeting with someone he knew. "A tantric yogi," he said. "He might be able to help. Where are you staying?"

We gave Rashmi our hotel information and he agreed to send a message with the details. He even promised to send his cousin along to take us so we would be sure to find the place. That evening we returned to the hotel to find a message and the cousin, Ratti, who focused mostly on chewing the betel leaves he kept tucked inside his bottom lip. They stained his teeth red and he dabbed at his mouth every few moments with a white handkerchief. Ratti told us that the tantric yogi was about to perform a ceremony and we had to hurry, and though he spoke politely and climbed into the rickshaw without complaint, he didn't appear to be in a particular hurry to go anywhere and I imagined he had other ways he would have preferred to spend his evening.

Our progress had been disrupted by a marching band procession and we'd been forced to the side as a parade of musicians in full regalia marched somberly down the road. I watched, unbelieving, as the musicians in bright white uniforms with blue and gold bandolier sashes and oversized military caps stomped toward us. Just before them, two gloomy middle-aged men dressed all in white pedaled a bicycle-powered cart hauling an enormous diesel generator that coughed and sputtered dark smoke into the air. Thick cables stretched behind the generator and linked three dozen marching pairs of men and women, each hoisting above their heads a large hooplike target of concentric circles glowing with maybe forty red and yellow lightbulbs, like electrified picket signs at a protest. I had no idea what they were. So frequently on this trip I would begin to feel as if I had a grasp on this new place, as though I were becoming one of those world-savvy travelers who could ease effortlessly into a new culture. But then, invariably, something like this marching band and its phalanx of electrified-sign bearers trudging through the night would come along and scrape away any sense of familiarity I had found.

"This is a wedding party!" Dabbu shouted over his shoulder. After the card trick the other day, he had shown us where he usually parked his rickshaw and offered to be our driver during our time in Varanasi. He nodded along with the music as a man marched passed us, morosely pounding the bass drum slung over his chest. Another man blew forcefully into a trumpet, but the sound was lost in the general din of the band, the grind of the generator, and the honking of the traffic, which had not let up despite the late hour. No one smiled.

"It's one hell of a party," I shouted back. "Why are they all so sad?"

"It's late," Dabbu replied, as if that explained everything. We made slow progress for five minutes as the parade kept coming— an unending stream of motorcycles, light bearers, marching musicians, and cyclists. Overhead the moon was almost full.

I had agreed to this meeting without really knowing what to expect, and as we drove, the words "tantric" and "yogi" rolled uncomfortably around in my imagination. Before leaving for India I knew nothing about tantra other than its vaguely erotic associations and some frankly impressive rumors about the musician Sting. After an uncomfortable conversation with a surprised Rashmi, I learned that in India, tantra is an ancient tradition of meditation techniques and spiritual practices. He thought it would be relevant to my search for magic because many of its adherents claim that tantra imbues them with certain powers that could only be described as magical—levitation, disappearance, the ability to perform miracles. Still, I had no idea what I was about to see.

Andy had not abandoned me on this admittedly dubious outing and he had the camera out and rolling as our rickshaw finally emerged from the parade and plunged back into the thick vein of traffic surging through the city. We turned down a dirt path that passed between two high stone walls and ran on like a secret passageway through the city. Eventually we emerged onto a quiet street, then turned down another. We were well off the main road now. Finally, the rickshaw turned into a courtyard and Ratti looked down at a piece of paper to confirm the address. Dabbu turned off the engine and we got out.

Four-story apartment buildings ringed the courtyard—all dark—and a concrete staircase led up to the building in front of us. Andy pointed the camera at me and said, "Nate, what are we doing?"

"We're outside an apartment building somewhere in Varanasi, about to meet with a tantric yogi. I think he's going to perform a ceremony. Someone gave us this address. Now we're here." Just saying it out loud made me realize how absurd the situation really was. I was in an unfamiliar city inside a foreign country on the other side of the planet, about to walk into this abandoned-looking apartment building to watch someone do God knows what, all because a film producer I didn't know thought it might be helpful. Navigationally, my closest reference point was the hotel, but I was at least a thirty-minute rickshaw ride through the dark from there and I couldn't even point in the direction of the hotel within 180 degrees of being right. For all practical—and even all theoretical—purposes, I was completely lost.

Ratti walked up the staircase and opened the door. It led to another staircase and we began to climb. The building felt like a parking garage, cold, hard, and dark, and our steps echoed up the stairwell ahead of us. I could hear doors closing as we approached. Bare electrical cables were stapled into the walls, which were covered in graffiti I couldn't read. We reached the fourth floor and walked down the hall to the last door. The bulbs in this part of the hallways were all broken, and the only light was a faint red glow coming from under the door, as though we had discovered our own private entrance to hell.

Ratti checked the paper again and then looked at me.

I knocked.

The man who answered wasn't naked, but he wore nothing but a cloth around his waist and wasn't happy to see us.

"What is it you want?" He had a thick beard and a mane of black hair. His eyes were hot and they darted first at me, then at Ratti, and then settled, glowering, on Andy's camera. "What is it you want?" he asked again. "Now you tell me."

By this point I was ready to go, but Ratti began to speak to the man in Hindi. The man looked at me very carefully and then back at Andy. They spoke for a full minute. Then, grudgingly, the man invited us inside.

A low table dominated the room, surrounded by stacks of books and papers. A large tome lay open next to a notebook covered in scribbly handwriting, and as we entered the yogi set them aside. Nothing there provided any immediate insight as to exactly what a tantric yogi did, but it appeared to include a great deal of reading. Above, an oversized portrait of a fat Indian man staring off into the distance hung on one wall. Another was dedicated to a platform or altar covered with ornate silver picture frames and a collection of stones arranged intricately on the red tablecloth. The air smelled like paperbacks and burning incense. The yogi asked us to sit on thick cushions next to the table.

"You people are very late," he said. "I understood you were coming to see the evening ceremony that must happen at sunset.

It is now well past sunset, and so I am uncertain why you have come at all. I will ask you again. What do you want?"

I looked at Ratti. Ratti looked at Andy. Andy looked at me.

So I began to talk. I spoke about my trip. I spoke about magic and disillusionment. I spoke about wonder and mystery and how I was on an adventure to expand my understanding of what a magician could be. "I met someone who thought I should speak to you," I said, "and I believe he told you we were coming. So we're here. If you have anything to say that might help me, I would be grateful. Otherwise, we'll go."

As I spoke I could see his hostility fading.

"You are a *choomantar*," he said. "A child's magician doing tricks. And those are the things of a very"—he searched for a kind way to say it—"Those are things of a lower level. Those magics performed by a *choomantar* distract from the real journey."

"What is the real journey?" I asked.

He leaned back and looked at the ceiling, trying to find a way to begin.

"Sometimes you feel as if you have everything," he said at last. "You have health, you have a good mind, you have money, you have prominence. You have all of this and still you are restless. This happens many times, does it not?"

He looked at me pointedly and I nodded.

"You came to my door and have come around the world to India because you are restless. Why? Why are you restless?"

I started to say something but he held up his hand.

"You are restless because you are looking for the truth and you cannot find it. You are restless because you cannot find the truth through your five senses alone. Your five senses show you the outside world, and you cannot find the truth in the outside world. And so you must go within."

I pointed out that the entire scientific process depended on our using the five senses to uncover truth in the outside world, but he held up his hand again.

"Our approach is also very scientific," he said. "We accept nothing on belief alone. We do not have faith in anything. We have no dogma. Ours is a very practical tradition. We pursue the mysticism of the world through direct experience of our own consciousness, and our tradition approaches this mystery scientifically."

"Can you give me an example?" I asked

He nodded, and over the next five minutes he described the process of creating actual miracles. How to leave your body and explore the world as pure consciousness, how to make yourself appear in two or three different places at the same time, how to ask a tree to produce a particular kind of fruit for you to eat and how to project the sun's rays through a glass of water and shine it on the tree so the fruit will materialize there on one of the branches. Calmly, deliberately, with the demeanor of a teacher trying to communicate a simple idea to a challenged student, he spoke about doing real magic.

One of the techniques of the modern magician is the very real skill of splitting your attention in half during a performance and allowing one half to recite the script for the show while freeing the other half for the secret workings of the illusion. One of the pieces in my show, for example, requires that I perform two calculations in my head while talking to the audience, all without allowing them to realize that they don't have my undivided attention. When I do it well it looks as if I'm just talking, but actually I'm crunching the numbers as quickly as I can with one half of my brain while allowing the other to run through the script on autopilot. Strangely, I can't do this in day-to-day life. It's a hard trick to practice because it relies on the adrenaline and power that you can access in the full flush of the moment in front of an audience but that is harder to find in the studio on a Tuesday morning when I'm rehearsing the show.

I mention this because as I sat and listened I could feel my mind doing the dividing trick, with one half following his conversation so I didn't miss anything and the other spinning as fast as possible, finding and rejecting ways of reconciling his claims with my own understanding of the world, trying to find some way to connect with his story.

I'm sure the effort showed on my face—as I said, it's hard to do when I'm not onstage—and my skepticism must have been obvious.

"We ask nothing to be held on faith," he clarified. "Suppose you came to me and said you had an elephant in your pocket. This sounds impossible. Your pocket is not large enough for an elephant and I should not believe you. I would have to see your pocket for myself, would I not?"

I nodded and said, "For me, the elephant in the pocket sounds as impossible as leaving my own body and flitting through the world with my consciousness."

"Yes. And it will remain that way until you see it for yourself. You must go within. And I must tell you that doing so is not child's play. Our tradition holds that most people use a very simple corner of the brain. Most of the power is not being utilized. Everybody has these hidden powers but they are sleeping—they are hidden. By our tradition we awaken those hidden powers. You have to unveil them, to realize them."

This was one of the strangest nights I'd had in a long time. I was a long way from making the coin disappear on the playground.

"Go within," he said. "There is a great magic within. Miraculous power is there."

~

"GO WITHIN." I kept hearing him say it for the rest of the night. We returned to the hotel an hour later and I took my notebook out to the courtyard and began to write. The moon had risen high in the night sky and there by the river the sounds of traffic were distant and low and I felt I had the city all to myself. "Go within," he had said, and on the ride back afterward, a few connections had come together and I wanted to write them down before I forgot.

On tour I had recognized that a magician can't actually create wonder. Granted, certain art forms are better than others at communicating different parts of the human experience— "Trying to write about music is like dancing about architecture," the saying goes—and a good magician is arguably in a better position than, say, a painter for giving an audience the experience of wonder. But it's not a direct cause-and-effect process. I can lead an audience down the hall to the doorway and open it for them, but the final step from "trick" to "magic" comes from them. And so while you put a lot of effort into creating the illusion in the first place, you spend as much effort guiding and shaping the audience's interpretation of that illusion during the performance so it feels less like a deception and more like an actual magical event.

And the connection I made on the way back to the hotel was that this is largely a matter of encouraging the audience to "go within." After a coin disappears, you don't want their attention to leap from one hand to the other hand, then to your sleeve— *Maybe it went up there*—then to your jacket, focused only on solving the problem of the missing coin. You want them to stay in that moment of astonishment as long as possible. You want them to dwell in it. You don't want them searching externally for a solution—you want them to believe in their bones that there isn't a solution, that it was magic they saw, and you want this conviction to resonate inside, deeper and deeper, so in the end the vanishing coin was nothing but a vessel for this inward experience of wonder, which was the real goal when you asked to borrow a quarter in the first place.

It's just like he said. You want them to go within.

The difference was that the tantric yogi used this process of deliberately steering his consciousness inward to see miracles, and I'd only ever been able to use it in a magic act. What the hell was he talking about with the fruit on the tree, by the way? I was trying to keep an open mind, but I didn't know what to make of his claims of actual magical powers. But his last thought resonated with me. *Go within, there is great magic within, miraculous power is there.* I had known this for years. I had known since age nine that the simple mechanics of a vanishing coin trick couldn't account for the visceral, powerful responses of the people who saw it. Clearly the coin had tapped into something internal. And the tantric yogi said there was more there to find.

~

THE NEXT MORNING I walked through the narrow section of street just before the open-air bazaar and a merchant stepped out from his doorway and raised his hand. "Magician, magician." He beckoned me over.

"Tell me, is your magic real? Are your powers genuine?"

Careful, here.

"I am a magician," I said, "not a prophet. I do magic tricks to create the experience of magic, but I don't have magical powers."

His face crumpled. "Magician, you have taken all of my hope. You have given it to me and then taken it all away."

It was time to go.

This wasn't the first time I had been recognized on the street as the magician visiting from America and I was worried about being too conspicuous. The other day by the river I had acquired a gaggle of hangers-on who had seen me do magic and wanted to see more, and I had a hard time convincing them I was done performing. I didn't want to have to duck the police again. Also, I had been speaking with people about magic in India and had heard a common suggestion: "Go north." Apparently the Himalayas were home to many who professed to have magical abilities, and if I wanted to learn more I should travel in that direction. Some recommended Nepal, some Assam to the northeast, and others suggested I go north of New Delhi.

But how? The trains were booked for the next two days and we were looking for other options. We called Rashmi for advice.

"I am going north on business, to Rishikesh," he said, "and you are welcome to join me." We looked at our map. Rishikesh was a few hours north of New Delhi—perfect. Rashmi gave us

the name of a café. "Can you meet me there tomorrow afternoon at one o'clock?"

When I'm on tour in America I like the simplicity of fitting
everything I need to live into one bag—clothes, books, freeze-
dried dinners, a few packets of instant coffee—with all of the
extraneous clutter pared away out of necessity. In India I had
even less. As we left the hotel, everything I owned for twelve
thousand miles in any direction fit into my green hiking pack
and the little blue bag we used for camera gear. My bag contained
an extra T-shirt, an extra pair of pants, a change of underwear, a
few pairs of socks, a handful of books—Saint-Exupéry's *Wind,
Sand and Stars*, Thomas Merton's *New Seeds of Contemplation*,
the copy of *Net of Magic* that had started this whole adventure,
and a few others. I had a toothbrush, toothpaste, a month's
supply of antibiotics, and a stick of deodorant. This last item
was mostly useless as I hadn't washed either of my T-shirts since
arriving and both had suffered. Andy, who had been traveling
like this for years, looked similarly run-down.

We were both unprepared and wildly underdressed, then,
for the pristine, oversized white Escalade that pulled up in front
of the café the next afternoon. Rashmi rolled down the window.
"Are you ready? Climb in."

GO NORTH

NINE HOURS LATER we were still driving north and I
stared out the window of the Escalade at India, which was
just there on the other side of the glass. The sun had set an hour
ago. The sky was open and the world was dark and the road felt
like a bridge suspended above an abyss. Rashmi slept in the
passenger seat in the front and Andy gazed out the window on
his side of the car. This was his third year away from home.

"Do you get used to all of this?" I asked.

"You mean the sky?"

"Yeah, the sky. And also driving across India through the
night in a giant white Escalade with a stranger."

Andy sat for a moment and I wondered if he wasn't going to
answer. "Yes," he said finally. "You get used to it."

"Is that a good thing?"

"It makes it more comfortable. I think you can get used to
anything."

"So how do you make your adventure feel like an adventure
again?" I asked.

"You go to India with a crazy American magician and travel
across the country looking for magic."

"So this is new, then?"

"Yes, this is new."

On tour everything felt the same: the airports, the airplanes, the hotels, the venues. For a while, the shows were the exception, but I had gotten used to them, too, and in the end, everything blurred together. I could sleep my way through a tour without ever really needing to pay attention. You could do that for a lifetime if you weren't careful. Now on this trip everything was new again, but how long could that last? Surely the answer wasn't simply to keep running away to something new. If searching for wonder was just a more interesting way to talk about novelty, all of this was a waste of time. The goal wasn't to run away from home, but to find what I was looking for and bring it home with me.

"When are you going to go home?" I asked.

Andy looked out the window.

"I am home."

∿

WHEN I WOKE it was still dark but someone was knocking on my door and I wanted it to stop. I climbed out of bed and crossed the black room—thinking about cobras—and cracked the door. Rashmi stood in the hall, dressed for the day, looking as if he had never once in his life needed sleep. He looked at me, surprised.

"Ah, Nate. Are you okay?"

"What? Yes. What time is it?"

"Did you sleep?"

"I mean—yeah, a little, Rashmi, but we just got in four hours ago."

He nodded. "Four hours is good. Now, dress and come
outside. There is something you must see."

I had marveled over the past twenty-four hours at the way
Rashmi's orders were obeyed immediately by everyone he
encountered—waiters, gas station attendants, the Escalade driver,
the man behind the desk at the hotel last night—and now that I
was on the receiving end I sort of understood. He looked at me
as though the entire universe hinged on my ability to follow this
one simple command—to dress and come outside so he could
show me something. He had already moved down the hall and I
heard him knocking on Andy's door. "Andy. Andy. Are you
awake? Come out, we must go." I pulled on yesterday's T-shirt
and in five minutes we were all standing in the lobby of the
hotel.

Outside, the only real light came from the headlights of the
Escalade, which dominated the street, incongruous here and
maybe everywhere but Texas. Behind the wheel the driver sat,
crumpled and harassed. We drove past the shapes of buildings
visible only as gray silhouettes against the black and purple of
the predawn sky, but you could tell the sun was coming up
because as we drove east the sky looked lighter and you could
see the buildings on the side of the road more clearly.

We rode for twenty or thirty minutes and I dozed as we
drove, muddling the drive with dreams and making both far
stranger than maybe they really were. How long had I known
Rashmi? A couple of days? I got the sense that he liked the idea
behind our trip and wanted to share his country with us, and I
imagined that in forty years or so I might feel the same about
two young adventurers visiting the United States from India.
Still, I barely knew him.

The car slowed and parked at the side of the road. We got out and I looked around. A low sandstone wall ran along the street and behind it a row of two-story buildings blocked out most of the view. The air was heavy and already warm, and I was still mostly asleep as Rashmi led us through a gap in the wall and disappeared down a sidewalk running between the buildings.

I didn't know what we were doing or where we were going. I wondered mostly about breakfast, and when I could go back to sleep. Someone nearby was cooking something, and I hoped the sidewalk would lead to a tea stand or a restaurant that served those pancake rolls we'd had the other day. I was thinking of lying down on the worn-thin mattress of the hotel bed, or the backseat of the car, or even right here if we could just stop for a minute so I could get comfortable there on the ground by the wall. But we walked on between buildings, moving downward, and then abruptly the buildings ended and the sidewalk emptied onto a broad courtyard, and time stopped.

The night before, we had driven north across what felt like a vast and unchanging plain and arrived late, unable to see anything beyond the closest streetlight. Now I looked out across the Ganges and saw the foothills of the Himalayas rise directly from the opposite riverbank and brighten as the sun peeked through a low valley in the hills. The sun caught the morning mist as it rose from the river and a thousand points of flashing light leapt and sparkled across the surface. It warmed the stones in the courtyard and the skin on my arms and face and turned the entire world a thick, heavy, incandescent gold. Everything was yellow, buttery, and radiant.

Rashmi stood at the edge of the water, hands held together behind his back as he looked out over the valley. Andy had his camera out. An old monk in an orange robe was ascending the stairs from the river. He climbed slowly, deliberately, and when he reached me he bowed. I bowed in return.

A gentle breeze was moving now, and I sat on the steps leading down to the river to watch the rest of the sunrise. Rashmi bent down by the river's edge, cupping his hands and filling them with water. He stood and poured the water over his head. He did this several times and then sat down beside me.

"Are you going to get in?"

"In the river? Are you serious?"

"Nate," he said, "I am serious."

A man stood knee-deep in the river with his eyes closed, his hands open and upturned. Another crouched almost fully submerged with just his head above the surface.

I don't remember what I was thinking. It wasn't a yearning for renewal or spiritual enlightenment so much as a realization that you don't travel from Iowa to the other side of the world and then *not* get in the river. If you're going to go, go all the way. So I stepped into the water—fully clothed—and began to walk forward. The water was cold but the sun was warming the air and still sparkling off the surface of the river, as if I were walking into a pool of light. I could feel the pull of the current. I was aware of my entire body, shivering and alive, and I wasn't tired anymore. I was wide awake.

∼

IT'S EASY TO go through a day without ever really waking up—to look without seeing, to listen without hearing, to live in the story you tell yourself about the world rather than the world itself. It sounds obvious when I say it but this is just because it's so common. We assume an overfamiliarity with the world around us that maybe makes it easier to live from day to day but harder to see things as they are.

I had seen sunrises before, of course, but that morning in the river it didn't feel like the same familiar yellow disk hauling itself up once again for another day. I felt that I was seeing it for the first time, perhaps because I was such a long way from home. I was far, far away from the life I had learned to live and this forced me to pay attention all the time—to my surroundings, to the people around me, to everything. I was off balance, and in an effort to regain stability I was constantly looking, searching, taking it all in. I wondered if India felt more "magical" simply because I was paying closer attention. I had no patterns or routines whose familiarity could insulate me from the world. When you wade shivering into the frigid water of the Ganges as the sun arches up and over the foothills of the Himalayas and lights everything up in gold, you have no choice but to snap back to the present, and stay there. For a second, nothing else matters. Your mind focuses sharply on the immediate—here, now— and for a moment it's impossible to think of anything else.

This is worth remembering. On tour, and in life in general, distraction is the rule rather than the exception. I'm always doing one thing, thinking about another, and ignoring a long list of other projects, people, ideas, responsibilities, and obligations that need my attention. At home my mind is fractured, divided, running a few different problems at once, and when I do lock in and focus on one thing, it's not long before I begin to worry that I really should be attending to something else.

This makes it almost impossible to really see anything. There's no time. And if there were time, it would come at the expense of something or someone else who also needs that time. The result is a fragmented, fractured life, where I could be surrounded by all the wonder in the world and not have any clue it's there.

I wondered how Katharine was getting along. How long had I been gone? Two weeks? Three weeks? Just over three weeks.

I closed my notebook and put it back in my bag. Andy and I had found a restaurant in the middle of the city for a late lunch and I'd spent an hour writing, and now that the hottest part of the day had passed we crossed over a high pedestrian suspension bridge that united the two sides of Rishikesh, which straddled the river and climbed the hills on both sides of the Ganges. Andy had the camera out and we planned to shoot some footage for his documentary as we explored the city. Maybe I'd do some magic, maybe we'd just walk around. It'd be easy, I thought.

As we walked I saw a cow—no, a bull—ahead, moving through the throngs of people who quickly cleared a path. He ambled along, clearly in no hurry, and Andy stopped to film the bull meandering down the sidewalk. I went ahead, keeping my eye out for a tea stand but mostly just enjoying the view of the river. The Ganges was stunning—wide and fast, the gold from that morning now replaced with a deep green and blue. The hills on either side rose abruptly from the water's edge and stood high above the city. The sky was clear, the air was fresh, all was well.

I'd been seeing monkeys all day, alone or in small groups, usually on the tops of buildings. Now I noticed one of them sitting on a fence on the edge of the sidewalk. This one sat alone, taking the world in, and when I walked by I sort of waved and said, "Hello, monkey." He screamed—a deep, angry shriek, improbably loud, and then he puffed up his chest, bared his teeth, and let me have it again. I took a step back, thinking I could just slowly move away, but this emboldened him and he started after me. Three or four other monkeys heard the call from the other side of the street and joined the chase in a dead run. I took off.

Andy was still with the bull, but because he intended to film some magic that day I wore a wireless radio microphone, and I knew that he could hear everything I said in his earpiece. The video recording sounds like this:

"Andy! Fuck! Andy! I'm being chased down the street by a pack of monkeys. Holy fucking shit! I don't know what I'm going to do!" There's a pause here and the sound of heavy running. Then, more quietly, "Andy, I'm hiding in a doorway at the end of an alley and the monkeys have me cornered. One of them has only one arm. I know you can hear me, and I don't know what to do."

A moment later from my vantage point in the doorway I saw a large, determined man enter the alley, making low grunting noises and banging a stick on the ground as he advanced. Behind him Andy was laughing uncontrollably, leaning against the wall for support, unable to move or speak. The monkeys dispersed, and I thanked the man for his help. For the rest of the afternoon, Andy would periodically stop whatever he was doing—talking, eating, filming—and dissolve again into laughter.

~

THE NEXT AFTERNOON I sat on the floor of a dimly lit room inside an ashram high in the hills above Rishikesh, waiting. Outside the door I could see the shade from the leaves of the massive Rudraksha tree at the center of the compound, and beyond the tree to the high stone walls that cloistered this place from the rest of the world. "He will be one moment more," said Laksuri, a woman in her midfifties who studied here. I'd met her the day before when she saw me performing magic in town shortly after the monkey incident and she invited me to the compound so I could show an illusion to her teacher. "It's marvelous," she said. "He will be very interested to speak with you."

Laksuri looked like Joan Baez and spoke with such authority and conviction that I couldn't imagine her as a student. She had left a successful career in law and moved to Rishikesh to study at this ashram, and even in a lifetime spent in the good company of cats I have never seen anyone more completely at peace with her lot in life. Laksuri divided her time between study, meditation, and contemplation of the Ganges, which she held in sacred adoration. "It is the lifeblood of all northern India," she explained, "and in her swirls and eddies you can see deeply into the mysteries of the world." She had been shocked, I think, and delighted to learn about my morning immersion in the river, and she spoke to me about the Ganges as if all the spiritual power of that body of water had instantly flooded and suffused every corner of my being. "You are never the same after you bathe in the Ganges," she said, looking at me as if we shared this secret understanding. "You know. You can feel it."

Her teacher entered the room.

He was younger than I expected—late forties, maybe, with a long black beard, gold-rimmed glasses, and eyes that sparkled behind them. He moved slowly and serenely but with an air of withheld power as if he carried some tremendous inner momentum, and I flinched when he sat down. He turned toward me and bowed slightly, closing his eyes, and I returned the bow. He spoke to Laksuri, and after he finished she translated.

"Maharaji has just returned from the mountains where he has been alone for several days. He wants me to convey that you are welcome here."

I nodded. "Thank you."

"Now I will tell him why you have come to India," she said, and as she spoke he studied me, seriously but not unkindly. Finally he began to speak, and I waited for the translation.

"There are people in India—singhs, or holy men—who produce 'holy ash' by trickery and present it as a miracle," he said. "Many people see this and find it unbelievable and amazing, but anyone with an education knows that if you put mercury and silver together the product of that chemical reaction will be this 'blessed ash.'"

"It's a trick," I clarified.

"Yes," he said. "It's a trick."

He told me that those who focus on miracles miss the point completely. "But," he offered, "if there is virtue in that trick, it's that it allows a moment of 'wow'—of wonder, and if you go deeply into that moment of wonder you might for one moment look inward, and see the wonder of your true self."

Yes! I thought. *This is it exactly!* Here again was this thought of using magic to go within, of looking through a trick rather than simply at it, but he had added something. *The wonder of your true self.* What did he mean by that?

"Why don't you show him the magic," Laksuri said.

I took a five-rupee coin from my pocket. My hands went through their motions and the coin disappeared.

The teacher leaned back and looked at me over the rims of his glasses. He said something to Laksuri.

"He wants to see another," she said.

I took two rubber bands and held them on my fingers. Magic happened.

Another half reaction—a tilt of the head, a slight widening of the eyes, but no break in his composure. He spoke to Laksuri again.

"He wants to see one more, if you can."

One more. I went to my backpack and came back with a spool of thread. I unraveled an arm's length and slowly, deliberately broke it into eight or nine pieces, holding each one up for his examination. He nodded throughout the process, following carefully, like a bank teller double-counting a handful of ones.

I gathered all the broken pieces of thread, rolled them into a ball, and then slowly, slowly unraveled it. The thread wasn't broken anymore.

He smiled. Then he laughed. He took off his glasses, still smiling, and looked at me as he polished the lenses on his robes. He began speaking, but this time he faced me as Laksuri translated.

" 'It's very beautiful,' the Maharaji says. 'What you have done is very beautiful, but there is something you must understand.' "

They spoke to each other again, as if clarifying a point. He praised me for the immense amount of work that must have gone into the practice of the tricks, and the concentration and care it must take to make them feel real for the audience. But he suggested that I was using those talents in the wrong way. He told me I was like a young child who had been given a dollar

and wasted it on candy rather than buying something important. "At this stage, you are only using your dollar for applause."
You shouldn't use it for a performance, he said. "It should be
utilized for something higher inside you."

He leaned toward me and once again removed his glasses.
This time he spoke to me in halting, careful English—taking
his time to choose the right words and turning to Laksuri for
help only when he couldn't find them.

"Everything is magic," he began, spreading his arms wide,
"and magic happens everywhere, but we are not ready to see it.
We don't have the eyes to perceive it or the ears sensitive
enough to hear it. What is more amazing than the fact that the
tree outside this door began as a little seed and has grown into
this huge tree which has millions of leaves and twigs, each one
different and unique? Isn't that magic? Isn't that 'wow'? It is a
miracle that we are all sitting here and discussing this. It is
a miracle you have come, and that we are all sitting together."
He said it again slowly. "This is a miracle."

He paused.

"But we never speak about our life like this," he said after a
moment. "We want our miracles on the outside." He raised his
fingers and rubbed them together, mockingly, sprinkling imaginary holy ash on the floor.

~

WE WANT OUR *miracles on the outside*, he had said, as if this was
ridiculous, misguided, missing the point.

You may find wonder in the sunrise or the stars in the sky at
night. You may find it on a mountaintop, or in the unexpected
kindness of a stranger. You may find it in a book, or a film, or in

that ecstatic, overpowering moment at a concert when the band blows the roof off the building. In each instance you become aware that the parts don't quite add up to the majesty of the whole. So what's the extra piece? Where does that come from?

Clearly, it comes from you. If you can find wonder in all of these disparate places, the common denominator in all of those experiences is *you*. Inside. Within.

I thought back to that night when my parents took me out into the middle of the cornfields to stare up at the Milky Way and watch the meteor shower. I remember marveling at the unimaginable vastness of the universe, certainly, but also recognizing in the face of that vastness the unique and even miraculous position we hold within it. There were the stars, the galaxies, and the gaping abyss of infinity rising up above us, reducing the earth and everyone on it to astronomical insignificance, and yet in all of that staggering distance we appeared to be the only ones who could think, act, hope, dream, or wonder. Think of that! Everything else in the universe is condemned to an eternity of *reacting*—of being pulled this way or that way according to the law of gravity and the other rules of physics. But here we are, living, loving, hoping, fearing, spurning, hating, thinking, reasoning—*acting*—all on our own. At that age I couldn't articulate it like this, of course, but that night under the stars and the meteor shower the paradox of being inconsequentially small and yet also somehow essential to the whole was impossible to ignore.

When I was a young magician I couldn't explain how something as simple as a coin trick could inspire such a powerful response. There may be such a thing as inherent wonder in distant stars or towering redwoods, but I knew better than anyone that there was none in the simple coin vanish—it was just a trick I had practiced in the bathroom. But now I considered that maybe the illusion gives us the experience of wonder because something in the act of beholding it scrapes away whatever has obscured this central mystery of our own existence. For just a moment we get to see it, and it fills us with fear, and also with joy.

At the end of our visit, the teacher led us out to the courtyard and we stood under the Rudraksha tree. He held out a bowl and presented Andy and me with the Tears of Shiva, small, hardened pods from the tree, considered valuable and holy in his tradition, in which they're used as prayer beads. Unfortunately, they also look very much like blackberries. As the teacher held the bowl toward us, Andy thanked him and popped one of the Tears of Shiva into his mouth.

"No!" the teacher cried. "They are holy!"

For the rest of the day I tried to turn Andy's mistake into an incident on the level of, say, being chased down an alley by a one-armed monkey, but whenever I mentioned the Tears of Shiva, Andy would begin to impersonate a monkey and then dissolve once again into laughter and that would be the end of it.

NOW WE PUT THE RIVER
TO SLEEP

THE NEXT EVENING Laksuri, Andy, and I drove a few miles downriver to the city of Haridwar and sat on the banks of the Ganges, watching families arrive for the *aarti* ceremony. Thousands of men and women led their children to vendors' stalls to purchase flowers and candles for the evening's proceedings. Bicycle rickshaws shuttled back and forth over a bridge, and on the other side of the river the tents of overnight pilgrims stretched along the bank. Slowly the occupants left the tents and joined the others at the water's edge. We sat far enough away that all of this solidified into the background, one with the setting sun and the high hills rising up from both sides of the river. Our corner of the riverbank was quiet. People sat in twos and threes to talk or silently look out over the water. At river level you can feel the immensity of the Ganges and it's easy to let your mind go far away as you sit and watch the current.

"First of all, we don't even consider the Ganga a river," Laksuri told us. "We worship her as a source of energy. She is the mother, and she feeds the entire north of this country. High in the mountains she is like a little girl, jumping and being very rough, running, skidding, and by the time she has reached us here she has grown up a little and is more calm."

A young girl of four or five years broke free from her father, ran to the river's edge, and lifted a handful of water into the air before letting it spill from her hands back into the river.

"You see that little girl," Laksuri said. "She's offering water to the river. It's a lovely gesture. What else can she give the river but the water she borrows from it?"

This was great, I'm sure, but I didn't really get it and I think she could tell that the meaning of this gesture, and perhaps of the river in general, was lost on me.

She spoke about her former life as an attorney in New Delhi—the good salary, the parties, the expensive car. A dream job—a dream life. And then she left it all behind. One afternoon on a business trip to Rishikesh she was driving home after a long day of meetings and had the overpowering impulse to swim in the river. She pulled over to the side of the road, took off her clothes, and waded in.

"It felt like an electric current was coming toward me from the river. The energy was just unbelievable, and at that time I was a complete nonbeliever in the power of the river to change or heal."

When she emerged, her life had changed. "I came back home and tried to eat the meat and drink the wine but I just couldn't touch it. In the river I had the clear vision, 'My life could be changed by one hundred and eighty degrees.' And now it has. And whoever comes to the river can change in the way they want. This is the magic of the Ganga."

As Laksuri spoke, a small audience gathered to hear her testimony, and maybe also because Andy had the camera out and was crouching and maneuvering for the best angle and looking

very much like a one-man TV crew. A young man of nineteen
or twenty approached. Laksuri bowed toward him and said,
"He is a Brahman—a priest—and he says he wants to bless you."

"What? Me?"

"Yes," she said. "Hold still."

He raised his hand to my forehead and whispered something. I didn't know what to do. I bowed. "Namaste," I said,
hoping this was appropriate.

Laksuri said something to him in Hindi, and I caught the
word *jadugar*, which I have discovered means "magician."

"Go on," Laksuri said to me. "Show him a trick."

I hesitated. When I made the coin vanish on the playground
as a young boy, some of the parents of the kids at school were
concerned—"One of the boys at school is practicing *magic!*"—
and one evening at a schoolmate's birthday party I was summarily
cornered by the boy's youth pastor and sternly warned about the
dangers of the magician's craft. "It's the work of the devil," he
said, and I could tell he really believed that. A handful of times
since then I have been approached after a show by members of one
church or another who want to discuss their spiritual concerns
with my work. And in one sense, I understand.

I understand because I'm aware of how easy it is for someone
in my positon to abuse the power of appearing to do the miraculous. Think of the spirit mediums in Houdini's day. Think
of the Godmen. The history of magic is filled with those who
have been willing to use their craft to dress themselves as gods
on earth, and we are all the poorer for it. But in a larger sense,
equating magic with sacrilege misses the point.

If a common ground exists between the worlds of faith and
reason, of theism and atheism, it lies in the experience of wonder.

A true believer and a committed skeptic can both gaze reverently at the night sky, or the towering redwood, or the screaming infant just new in the world, and find in that moment the humble, open sense of awe and interconnectedness with the universe that exists at the heart of both the religious and scientific traditions. Both skeptic and believer are capable of getting lost in the weeds of their own certainty, and both are capable of rising above it to stare unflinchingly at the brute fact of our own existence and to find in that awful and joyful reality the experience of gratitude—despite everything—and wonder.

Admittedly, this has nothing to do with card tricks. Magic can be used in a number of ways, some good, some bad, and most often, neither good nor bad. You can use magic tricks to entertain, to baffle, to deceive. But you can also use them to share the experience of wonder. There's an ongoing battle between magicians as to whether magic tricks are inherently artistic. I don't think they are, but they can be. Learning someone else's coin trick and doing it on the playground as a nine-year-old didn't require much artistic vision, but I spent years creating the lottery illusion. Magic can be art, and art can be sacred, and therefore magic can also be sacred. Magic may not have had its version of Beethoven's Seventh Symphony or Jackson Pollock's *Mural* yet, but that's not to say it couldn't happen. And if it did, it probably wouldn't be bombastic or overblown. It would be simple and direct. It would be honest and straightforward. And it wouldn't feel like a magic trick. It would feel true.

By this point an audience of maybe fifteen people had gathered to watch the Indian priest and the American magician. "Go on," Laksuri said again. "It's okay."

I showed him the rubber band trick three times. After the first time his face remained blank and impassive. I did it again, and a slow smile spread across his face. No one in the group yelled or screamed, but collectively they leaned in, moving closer, watching carefully.

One last time. Two rubber bands—one here, one here, then— Magic.

I heard Laksuri react with the rest of the crowd but I was watching the priest. He looked at my hands and then into my eyes. He bowed his head.

"Namaste."

⌒

EARLIER IN THE evening Laksuri had told me what I should expect from the aarti ceremony. *Aarti* is a word from the Sanskrit language that means "remover of darkness," and she described the ceremony as a way of thanking the holy river.

"People will buy flowers, put a little lamp on it, and release it into the river. Showing a light, burning a candle—these are symbols that say to the river, 'This is my energy and I got it from you. I offer it back to you in thanks.' And then because it is night and we all must sleep, we sing to the river. We sing the river to sleep, like a lullaby."

I am a secular magician performing secular magic and the aarti ceremony is an explicitly religious event. My evening in Haridwar was not unlike an Indian magician unaware of the tenets of Christianity traveling to America and wandering unknowingly into a Christmas Eve nativity service—the candles, the incense, the singing of "Silent Night"—and finding in that moment the experience of wonder. I lacked the language, the knowledge, and the context to take in the aarti ceremony as it was intended. I missed many things and misinterpreted the rest. I saw it all as an outsider.

But it was pure magic.

In the years since that night I have wondered if this outsider perspective allowed me to appreciate the power of the moment more viscerally than someone who knew the meaning, because anyone who knew the meaning would have to decide how they felt about it, making their experience at least partly analytical instead of purely emotional. I think of this at the Nativity service every year. I know the Christmas story and the theological claims presented by the story, and so my experience of that night depends as much on my relationship with that story and those claims as it does with the service itself. As we pass the candles and sing the familiar carol, I have to consider what the story means to me.

Contrast this with our imaginary Indian magician, still stunned and disoriented from the culture shock of traveling from India to Iowa and thankful mostly to sit in the dark in peace for a moment and take in the spectacle of Christmas Eve. *Peace be with you*, his neighbor in the church pew says, and though he can't understand the words, he senses the welcome in the phrase and accepts with thanks and solemnity the lighted candle passed to him. As the lights are dimmed and the candles cast shadows on the vaulted ceilings, this gathering of farmers, doctors, teachers, and factory workers stands and sings together the quiet, stirring melody of "Silent Night." What would our Indian magician take from this moment? The theology would be lost on him, certainly, and some of the elements of the service would likely baffle him—the crucified Christ on the wall, for instance, and the taking of wine and bread in communion—but even when the particulars of the moment are removed the overarching, overpowering sense of the numinous remains.

This, at least, was my experience that night when I joined the thousands and thousands of pilgrims who had traveled across the country to the banks of the Ganges in Haridwar to sing the river to sleep. That night the mythology behind the ceremony was invisible to me, so all I saw was the ceremony itself.

~

WHEN THE SETTING sun disappeared behind the hills on the opposite bank the first fire sprang up in the darkness, and within five minutes every candle, torch, and bonfire for half a mile on either side of the bridge was burning. The river glowed in the firelight. As we joined the throngs moving toward the ceremony I could see thousands and thousands of people crowding closely along both sides of the river. In many places the bank had been stair-stepped down to the water with stone platforms, accommodating the massive audience like an amphitheater rising from the river's edge on each side.

We got separated almost immediately. Andy disappeared with the camera. Laksuri vanished into the crowd. I was in a throng of people rushing to get close to the river and allowed myself to be swept along without knowing where I was going or what I would find. I quickly abandoned my initial hope of working my way to a raised platform to view the proceedings from above. I was down in the middle of it, on the ground, one of the thousands moving toward the river. The air was hot and thick with the smell of sweat and burning oil. The crush of people, the heat, the sounds, and the smells all joined together like an intoxicant. On my right, a loudspeaker blared the prerecorded wail of a woman singing a warbling melody, high and pleading. On my left, a man about my age dressed all in white stood with his eyes closed, face upturned, his voice rising and falling in a deep, rhythmic chant.

Above it all rose the sounds of the crowd, which appeared both as a churning mass of moving candlelight and song and also a series of distinct individuals, cast in my memory as a progression of fantastic images. A man struggled with a large torch overloaded with fuel oil and dripping liquid fire on the ground as parents pulled their children out of his way. The crowd surged and he was gone. A grandmother carefully carried a bowl made from folded leaves and filled with flowers and a burning ghee candle. She knelt to present it to her delighted grandchildren. They carried it away together toward the river, each reaching in over the others to position a hand under the bowl, not wanting to miss out. The crowd shifted again. When it opened I stood directly before a girl of nine or ten holding a large silver tray covered with coins and a burning flame rising four or five inches from a small bowl. An old man bowed before her and she anointed him with the fire, passing her fingers through the flame and then pressing them into his forehead. He raised his hands in thanks, and she turned to me. Again she passed her fingers through the fire. I bowed and felt her fingertips press firmly into my forehead. Then she was gone.

Eventually I reached the river.

On either bank the crowd pressed so closely to the water that the first few rows of people were partially submerged, some to their waist, some to their knees and ankles. A handful of children shepherded a fleet of leaf bowls filled with candles and flowers from the banks out into the river, celebrating each time the current took a bowl from their outstretched hands and carried it downstream. Dozens of these burning bowls floated down the river, and as they disappeared beyond the bend the children replaced them with others, creating an unending procession of floating candles sailing away into the darkness.

On both sides of the river a profusion of upraised torches and towering bonfires amid the crowd reflected off the flowing surface of the water, scattering the light in every direction. I no longer stood on the banks of a river; I was suspended in space, with light above, below, and around me, flickering in the darkness. The moon hung low in the sky—a final light above the bonfires, torches, and candles, as if the universe had conspired to create one perfect moment and decided at the last minute to go all out and include the moon.

I was standing near the edge of the water when the singing began. Until then the music had been scattered, with some people singing one song and some another, and others not singing at all. But then everyone—some five thousand people—began singing the same song, quietly, and a current passed through the crowd.

This was magic.

I don't know how else to say it. This was one of the most magical moments of my life. This was the meteor shower in the night sky and the sound under the piano. This was awe. This was wonder.

A family stood next to me—a boy, maybe four, his older sister, and their parents, all quietly singing the death knell of everything I had ever done as a magician. This was more amazing. This was better. Take my best moment onstage, the

lottery illusion at the bar, or the coin vanishing on the playground, and this night raised up with song and moon and fire
wins every time. This felt the way magic should feel. This felt
true.

I had been trying for years to identify exactly why so much
of the magic in my culture disappointed me, including my
own. The real issue is that so often, magic doesn't feel true. It
doesn't make you say "Aha! Yes! I remember that! I knew that
once." Years ago I came across the idea that truly great works of
art instruct less than they remind. When you listen to Bob
Dylan's *Time Out of Mind* or walk through Frank Lloyd Wright's
Unity Temple in Oak Park, Illinois, or watch old videos of
Michael Jordan at the height of his powers, the experience is
not one of discovering something new but rediscovering
something old within yourself. These pieces of art and feats of
athleticism are bigger than the artists' personal experience. They
resonate on a universal human level, and we find in them pieces
of our own selves that we may have forgotten in the daily
business of living.

I didn't understand the words of the song. I didn't know the
meaning of the lights or the candles. None of the specific
theology of the moment was available to me. It didn't matter.
Whatever it was that rose up from that particular combination
of sound, fire, darkness, and water transcended theology. It was
bigger and more fundamental. Like real magic.

At some point someone handed me one of the bowls. It was
heavier than I expected, folded together from thick green leaves
and filled with loose flower petals and a narrow burning candle
at the center. The man who gave it to me was thin and old,
with a white beard and a bald head. He nodded and motioned

to the river, smiling. I bent down and pushed the burning bowl into the water. It clung to the shore, moving slowly downriver, until a young boy splashed over and piloted it out into the current. I watched it join the other lights, floating, bobbing, rushing away, until it curved around the bend in the river and disappeared.

I sat on the steps and closed my eyes. Though it must have happened, I have no memory of finding Andy or making it back to the hotel. For me, the night ended there on the steps by the river, listening.

THE POET

THE NEXT MORNING, I woke up early and went out to find breakfast. I'd noticed a noodle shop doing brisk business just down the block and thought I could probably get something and bring it back to the room. The sights and sounds of the night before by the river had bled through into my dreams and I was having a hard time deciding where the one ended and the other began, which made the whole thing feel all the more surreal and magical. I wondered how I could share that experience when I got home, and whether I could use any of it in my work as a magician—not overtly so the audience could see it, but under the surface, as subtext, so it looked like a magic show but felt like a night on the Ganges with the Himalayas just out of sight beyond the foothills. At the moment this all felt nebulous and vague but I thought I could make it work.

I'd also been thinking about the teacher's comment that I was using magic for the wrong reasons. He was right; I had been. I remembered the disgust I had felt during the show in Milwaukee—when all of my original intentions had fallen away during the grind of touring and I'd realized it all at once in front of everyone in the audience. But I thought my original intentions were pretty good. I had discovered early on that you could use magic to say something valuable and share it with the audience rather than simply putting the tricks up on display, and that morning I started thinking about new ways I could make that work on a practical and technical level during a performance.

This was the first time I had really thought about my work since leaving home. I'd done magic for people I'd met, of course, but this was always informal—more of a way for me to get people talking about magic than any desire on my part to put on a show. A show is a different thing entirely. But this was a Thursday, and if I'd been home I almost certainly would have been working. With the time difference it would have been mid- to late evening in the States, so I probably would have been onstage at that very moment. I tried to decide whether I missed it, but in the end I just got the noodles and went back to the room.

Rashmi had to drive to New Delhi and I didn't know what else to do in Rishikesh, so later that morning we all piled into the oversized Escalade one last time. Before leaving for India, I had envisioned my transformation into one of those worldwise vagabonds with a well-worn backpack, a sheaf of train tickets jammed into the outer pocket, and shoes tattered from miles and miles of walking, hoping for a ride from a stranger. Much of this had come true. My shoes were dusty and both of my T-shirts looked exhausted, but I had spent more time in a luxury SUV than I'd anticipated.

~

A FEW HOURS later we arrived in New Delhi and said goodbye to Rashmi. He climbed back into the giant white Escalade and vanished into the swirling, rushing torrent of New Delhi traffic.

We checked in to a guesthouse and Andy went to his room to make a phone call. An hour later this same river of traffic deposited a blue-and-tan minivan in front of the guesthouse and I met his friend Amit for the first time. "Andy!" he bellowed, sliding from the front seat and stomping across the median like a large, friendly bear. He grabbed Andy's shoulders and looked him squarely in the face. "I am glad to see you again." Amit looked like a Prussian Hussar, spoke like a military commander, and wore a large handlebar mustache without a trace of irony. He turned to me and snapped out a greeting.

"You must be the magician." I nodded.

"I have a great fondness for magicians," he said. "They're the only people crazier than poets. Welcome to New Delhi."

Amit, I knew, was a poet. A famous poet. In fact, the poet laureate of New Delhi. He and Andy had become friends during Andy's previous time in India and he had agreed to show me around. He was bright, forceful, fierce, and welcoming. I liked Amit immediately.

"We must eat," he said, ushering us toward his van. "Get in."

One of the joys of traveling so far from home and work is that midday on a Thursday carries as few responsibilities as a Saturday or a Sunday at home, so after a large, late lunch we went to the park to sit on a bench and talk. The sprawling turf of the Lodhi Gardens carves out a green and quiet haven in the middle of the city, much like Central Park in New York, I suppose, but filled with monkeys, which I eyed with suspicion. They roamed, sometimes alone, sometimes in great galloping packs, and had grown so numerous and so aggressive in their relentless search for food that they had become a problem. Homes were robbed, businesses interrupted, and even New

Delhi's police headquarters was targeted for raids by these
marauding packs of Rhesus macaques, who descended on buildings like locusts on a crop of wheat and quickly exploited any
open windows or balconies. The solution, I learned, was for
home and business owners to employ larger monkeys, posted
and chained at vulnerable entry points to intimidate and frighten
away the smaller ones, like scarecrows who could throw their
own shit.

WE WALKED THROUGH the park and I told Amit that I was
trying to reconcile two different perspectives of magic I had
encountered in India.

The first was that magic is nonsense—*things of a very low
level*—and that everything has a rational, scientific explanation.
I heard this everywhere. But then, and sometimes from the
same people, I would hear firsthand accounts of feats that could
only be described as magical: spells cast on sisters, tantric yogis
flitting through the air as pure consciousness, fruit miraculously appearing on trees. India is known around the world as a
Land of Mystery. Now that I was here I understood why many
people were trying to shed this image, but then why was there
so much talk about magic?

Amit listened and then offered another interpretation of magic
in India. He spoke about magic as a way of honorably and ethi-
cally interacting with the unknown—in the world, in ourselves,
in those around us.

"To me, magic is all about understanding how human beings
bridge the gaps in the human condition. We are all born with a
great emptiness within us that needs to be filled, and we spend
all our time trying to fill that hole in ourselves. This is exhausting,

and it is a work we never finish. And so we will always have gaps between who we are and who we want to become."

At lunch Amit had ordered course after course for the entire table like a king, summoning the waiter again and again, sending dishes back when they weren't right, effusing praise and appreciation when they were. There he had been gregarious, commanding, a bon vivant, larger than life, like a character from a movie. Now he chose his words slowly and deliberately and the world around us faded away.

"How do we bridge those gaps?" he asked. "We bridge them with compassion, for ourselves and for others. We bridge them with faith, that all will be well in this world and maybe in the next. And we bridge them with magic."

Amit suggested that India truly was a Land of Mystery because it needed to be. "Here we have such extraordinary diversity— different languages, different religions, different peoples, divided in almost every way people can be divided—all jammed together and united under the Indian flag," he said. He explained that a sense of magic and a view of the world that allowed for the possibility of magic acted as a societal cushion to ease the tensions that come from such differences. "The more magic we have in our encounters with one another, the more we're able to deal with the differences between us," he said. "It's okay to be different, it's cool to be different. We don't have to understand each other to honor one another."

Amit also explained that this might be hard for an American to understand. In India, food shortages are frequent and the poverty rate is much higher than it is in America. "There were bread shortages in Moscow and the Soviet Union collapsed. You've heard the stories of the food shortages in India, but

where are the riots? Where are the massacres? It doesn't happen
here because of the magic of belief and the magic of faith."

I asked how he felt about the spiritual leaders who used
magic tricks to reinforce their teachings, like the gurus who
use sleight of hand to produce "holy ash." Again he suggested
that America's prosperity might make it hard for me to understand the issue clearly. "Even the most knowledgeable people in
India have spiritual leaders, or gurus. The production of 'holy ash'
you mentioned is very common. Let me ask you—does it matter
whether it's a miracle or just sleight of hand? Does it matter? If it
delivers relief to a person who has very little income, very little
savings, does it matter if it's actually a magic trick? If a magic
trick reduces a man's suffering in a real and tangible way, who
are you to tell him it's wrong, or that it's not true, or that it's just
a trick? Who are you to decide what is 'real' and what is 'fake'?
He prays and hopes for his burdens to be lifted or made a little
lighter and then—by magic—they are. Where's the trick in
that?"

The insinuation here was clear—*Take your righteous indigna-
tion and shove it.* I didn't know what to say. I'm not alone in
thinking that the Godmen are inexcusable—again, the Indian
Rationalist Association has been fighting a long-running war
against them for years. But it occurred to me for the first time
that the issue was maybe more complicated than I first assumed.

Amit's voice was still soft, but it had an edge now. "Come
down to the level of the street, Nate—the level at which our
billion-man society lives and survives in an orderly fashion here
in the heat and the dust. America has plenty of food and air
conditioning. Here you have people who are living much closer
to the earth and closer to the reality of shortage, and suffering.

"But despite all of the challenges of life in this country, look at the success of our democracy. There are nations right around the corner from us, next door in fact, that have no such success with democracy, and they have only one people and one language. In India we have a thousand faiths, a thousand tongues, and yet our democracy thrives. What else besides an awareness of magic could achieve this? I do not believe that there is a science or a wisdom alone that can take the credit."

Amit's assertion that belief in magic acted as a kind of cultural anesthetic didn't sit easily with me. But I recognized that this didn't make it wrong, either. I was coming to distrust my own ability to judge anything so far from my own under-standing, and in India almost everything was far from my own understanding.

Just before we got up to leave, Amit added one last thought.

"Magic—your magic, the magic of magicians—delights us because it gives us a moment of not knowing, an island moment of wonderment, and joy, and innocence. It reminds us that it's okay not to have all the answers or all the information—that we can move on with our lives anyway. And that we should, because we will never have enough information."

THE STREET MAGICIANS OF
SHADIPUR DEPOT

A BOY SITS ON the ground at the crossroads of a small village. Everyone has come to watch, and fifty people are gathered in a circle. The boy is at the center, blindfolded. Behind him, his father is sharpening a sword with a stone.

The father looks down the blade and then places the stone on the ground. The boy hears the sword on the stone, the stone on the ground, and the footsteps as his father approaches.

"Father?"

The father whispers into his son's ear. The boy lowers his head.

The villagers watch hesitantly, unmoving.

The father raises the sword and massacres the boy.

The butchery takes less than a minute and is done methodically and deliberately, completely without anger, as if slaughtering a lamb for the table. By the end the broken, bleeding body of the boy lies in the center of the road. Blood runs through the dust and the villagers step to the side to let the rivulets pass.

The father places the sword on the ground and tenderly picks up the body of his son. He places the boy on a large cloth and folds the edges of the cloth over the body. It is a small bundle. Blood begins to seep through the fabric.

The father begins to pace in a circle around the body. He whispers again, this time with force and urgency, as if casting a spell. He walks faster, speaking louder. He is shouting now; shouting in an unknown language with his hand outstretched toward his son. He cries out and falls to his knees. Then he is silent.

The cloth begins to move.

At first the villagers aren't even sure that it happened. Maybe the wind caught the cloth and made it shift. But there is no wind, and again it moved. Clearly it moved.

The cloth begins to unfold. The villagers are shocked to see that it is no longer soaked with blood. Then it falls away and the boy stands, miraculously unharmed, back from the dead. The blood is gone, the wounds are gone. The father raises his hands in triumph. The boy takes a bow.

An hour later—after the chaos and congratulations, after the end of the performance and the farewells of the villagers— the boy and his father walk down a road that disappears into the country. They are talking about magic.

The father learned the secrets from his father, who learned them from his father, stretching back in time for a thousand years, long before anyone can remember. Now he is passing them on to his son. No one knows where the secrets began— maybe they have always existed. Where did you learn this? My father taught me. That is all.

The secrets reveal the magic, and the magic is extraordinary— how to produce water from an empty bowl, how to breathe fire, how to cut your arm with a knife without showing pain, how to miraculously heal the wound. These feats are gritty and brutal, far removed from the sterile card tricks and stage illusions of the modern American magician. This is magic with mud on its boots, less a form of entertainment than an expression of the inescapable, everyday struggles of poverty, thirst, hunger, violence, and death. The massacre is the last illusion in the show, and its unflinching barbarity is a carefully constructed allegory of loss, overturned in the end by the power of the magician. It's Abraham and Isaac without the divine intervention—here, the boy just dies. Only after the weight of this tragedy has fully descended over the audience does the magician bring the boy back to life, and the miracle is not an expression of divine grace but rather a demonstration of the magician's own power—his ability to defy the rules of the universe and his victory over mortality, fear, frailty, and suffering, even if just for a moment.

This is how the illusions look to the audience—full of glory, tragedy, and triumph—but as they walk the father does not talk to his son about glory. When he speaks to his son he talks about the craft, the tools of the trade, the work. The tricks are a way to make a living. He speaks as if they are fishermen and he is teaching his boy to catch a fish—this is how you bait the hook, this is how you throw the line. But instead of catching fish they are creating magic, and step by step the boy learns to perform miracles.

In this way the boy and his father cross the country, performing in one village and then traveling to the next, moving along the ancient routes of their ancestors. Tomorrow they will come to another village and stage another performance, and soon they will rejoin their family and share the money they have earned.

Years later, when he has become a father, the boy passes the secrets on to his son, who in turn passes them to his son, and he to his, and this over and over for two thousand years until the father's name is Ishamudin and the son's name is Altamas and I am sitting on the floor of their home in a slum known as Shadipur Depot outside New Delhi.

Their family has become legendary in the world of magic—a nomadic tribe of Indian street magicians who have passed their secrets from father to son in an unbroken chain for more than three thousand years. I have traveled halfway around the world to meet them and I am watching a private performance of their ancient illusions. I have seen extraordinary things: fire breathing, needle swallowing, water produced from an empty bowl; and now they are about to perform one final illusion.

The father is sharpening a sword. His son stands before him, blindfolded. I have no idea what is coming.

~

BEFORE LEAVING THE U.S., I had sent a message to Lee Siegel, the author who inspired my trip to India. I wanted to know if he had kept in touch with any of the magicians from *Net of Magic* and if he could facilitate an introduction so I could meet them when I traveled to New Delhi. He responded with an offer to put me in touch with the leader of the tribe, and also a warning: *Shadipur Depot is a slum, and you can't just walk in and say hello.*

Amit had given me the same warning the day before when we sat on the bench in the park.

"There's this fine American phrase," he said. "It's pithy, it's to the point—the expression '*Oh shit.*' Shadipur Depot adds a whole new meaning to that expression. When you go there, suddenly you know what it means. It's a complete invasion of your entire aesthetic sensibility. There's no way you can come out of that without—"

He trailed off and thought for a moment.

"It's like going through one of Dante's books. In Shadipur Depot you come to a place where a child is studying right next to the lavatory, and is going to school, and getting grades. And on the other side of the lavatory a mother is cooking food. And it is a life. That's where they have their life. What a paradox the human condition is, because despite all that deprivation and poverty people still have a life."

THE DAY HAD started ordinarily enough. That morning I lay in bed at the guesthouse, not sleeping, watching through the window as the sky turned from dark to light and thinking about the day to come. Soon Amit would arrive with his van and we would go to Shadipur Depot to meet the magicians, but for a moment I lay there, listening to the city as the roads filled with traffic, the sun rose, and the day began.

An hour or so later Andy knocked on my door and we went to eat breakfast before our trip into Shadipur Depot. For the first time on the trip he looked afraid.

"How are you feeling?" he asked.

"Nervous," I said.

"Yeah."

"Have you ever done anything like this?"

"No," he said. "Not like this."

Amit arrived a few minutes later. He didn't want to take his van, so he parked it next to the guesthouse and called a taxi. We drove in silence for twenty minutes or so and then the driver stopped the taxi.

"Here you get out," he said.

"A few blocks farther, my friend," said Amit.

"No, you get out here," the driver replied firmly.

"Our destination is a few blocks farther on, my friend," Amit said again.

"No no. You will get out here."

Amit said something in a language I didn't recognize—not angrily, but with conviction. The driver looked at me in the rearview mirror and then back at the road. He drove on. Two minutes later he stopped and we got out.

"Okay Nate," said Amit, as he indicated the neighborhood across the street. "Shadipur Depot."

It looked as if it had been firebombed, like the pictures of Dresden after the war. A warren of ruined brick buildings had been patched together with sheets of corrugated aluminum. Layers and layers of garbage had been left everywhere to rot, or burn, or drift against the side of the buildings. The air was choked with smoke from the smoldering waste, but even the fumes of the burning trash could not mask the stench of human shit rising in waves from the open, flowing sewer. On one side of the street the crumbling brick husk of a two-story building had filled with its own rubble and mounded over with a mountain of accumulated trash, and a group of children picked through this garbage, stashing the more valuable discoveries into plastic grocery sacks tied to the end of sticks. Two of the little girls were completely naked. One of the young boys looked up and made eye contact— a haunted look, as though we had startled him: *Who are you? Why are you here? What do you want?* But that's not quite right. What was that expression? He gripped his sack of garbage.

Don't take this. It's mine.

We had arranged to meet Ishamudin on this particular corner on this particular day. We stood waiting, conspicuously, and as we waited Amit turned, watching, aware of everyone around us.

"This is it, right?" I asked after a moment.

"Yes," said Amit. "This is it."

I felt everyone watching us. The children sat and looked at us warily, having momentarily stopped their hunt through the trash. Two men broke off their conversation on the steps of a building across the road and now stared silently in our direction. Amit stared back. A woman carrying a large bundle of yellow cloth on her head crossed the road and then looked sharply up, noticing us, startled, before hurrying off. All around, I felt the day-to-day life in Shadipur Depot stop and take note of our arrival as we stood on the corner.

"There," said Amit a moment later. "That must be him." A man walked toward us from one of the side streets. He wore a bright yellow shirt and a gray vest that looked out of place in our burned-out surroundings. He looked more like a dad at a soccer game than a great magician.

"You are Nate?"

I nodded.

"My name is Ishamudin Khan. Welcome to my home."

Ishamudin led us down a path into the slum and I became lost almost immediately. The path was narrow and seemed to lead through houses as often as it led around them—we crossed a small courtyard, turned down a side passage, walked through someone's kitchen, turned onto another side street that also served as a hallway through one of the buildings, and descended a long staircase that somehow both started and ended at ground level. The narrow strip of sky overhead vanished frequently as we passed through tunnels, doorways, hallways, and buildings.

We passed a monkey chained to a wall and sleeping on a pile of cloth, and a man standing next to an upright oil barrel, working on a fire. We kept going. I stood to one side as a young boy—a toddler, really, no more than three years old—staggered down the hall carrying a baby. The two were practically the same size. The older boy smiled at me as he passed, carefully gripping his baby brother as he stepped across an open drain in the floor. They turned the corner and were gone.

We stopped when Ishamudin announced that we had reached his house. He opened a door and led us inside a dark, low-ceilinged room. It was filled with magicians.

Ishamudin introduced me to the group; then I sat silently as they spoke to one another. A plate of potato chips sat in the center. I would learn later that this was an extravagant gesture of welcome—potato chips for the American visitor—but at the moment I didn't know what to think. Amit was clearly uncomfortable. This made me uncomfortable.

Finally Ishamudin said, "I understand that you are a magician?"

"Yes."

"Could you show us one of your tricks?"

Of course. They wanted to see if I was any good.

In America, entrance to the various clubs and societies of magicians is sometimes contingent on a performance, to demonstrate that you've already put in the requisite time and commitment to the craft, and this group—quite rightly—wanted to verify the same. The potato chips indicated that their hospitality would be offered either way, but I wanted to talk to them about magic.

I gathered the group in a circle and removed the spool of thread from my backpack. Some illusions rely on subterfuge or technology, some rely on psychological subtlety and a mastery of the ability to manipulate the attention of the audience, but some illusions rely on nothing more than pure sleight-of-hand technique that cannot be faked, purchased, or obtained by any other means than standing in front of a practice mirror and putting in months and often years of work. I didn't know whether I could amaze this group of magicians, but I wanted them to know that I had chops.

I broke a three-foot section of thread from the spool and held it at my fingertips so that everyone could see. They were watching very closely. Slowly and deliberately, I broke the piece of thread into four or five smaller pieces, handing each piece to a different magician to demonstrate that the thread was actually broken. When I had performed this for the teacher at the ashram in Rishikesh he had watched sharply, trying to catch any false move. But I felt a warmth from this group and remembered that magicians love magic tricks more than anyone else.

"Roll the pieces into a small ball," I said. Amit helped with the translation, and one of the magicians collected the broken pieces and rolled them together.

"Watch this." I retrieved the ball of broken thread and pulled slowly on two of the loose ends. The magicians began to smile. As I pulled on the string, the ball continued to unroll and within seconds they saw that the thread had been completely restored. Laughter, applause, handshakes, pats on the back. I'm sure that any of them could have performed a similar feat easily, but my execution had been flawless and their reserve fell away.

We spoke for an hour about magic, first in generalities about our careers and then about specific illusions. One of the tricks in my show has its roots in a traditional piece of magic from India and they watched—with amusement, I think—as I demonstrated my version of an illusion that has been handed down from father to son in their tribe for millennia. I passed out a handful of sewing needles for inspection and unwound another length of thread. After gathering the needles I placed them on my tongue, closed my mouth, and swallowed. In my show this moment elicits groans, gasps, shrieks of disgust and dismay. Here, nothing. No response. I opened my mouth to show the needles were gone and they just waited. One man nodded politely. The same thing happened when I swallowed the length of sewing thread—no response. It was only when I pulled the thread back out of my mouth—now with all of the needles threaded along its length, dangling and glinting in the light—that they responded with any sort of enthusiasm.

"It's good," one of them offered—a young man about my own age who spoke no English but communicated with me through Amit. "You have good technique."

A pause.

"Would you like to see how we do it?"

I SAT ON the roof of Ishamudin's house across from an eighty-two-year-old man who was about to breathe fire. He opened his mouth to show that it was empty. Then he closed his eyes and exhaled smoke through his nose and the hair on the back of my neck stood up. The smoke hung lazily in the unmoving air and joined the smells of shit, filth, and garbage that rose from the ground and the open sewers and clung to the slum like flies on rotting food. The sun had been high in the sky for hours, days, years, and the bricks under my feet radiated a deep, ancient heat, as though they had never completely cooled from the kiln. The T-shirt I'd worn for the last month stuck to my back, thin and soaking. I was hot and thirsty, but at the moment none of this mattered.

Word of this performance had spread throughout the neighborhood and twenty or thirty people had crammed onto this patio to watch Ishamudin's father come out of retirement for one last show. At the sight of the smoke everyone jostled for a better view—children on shoulders craned their necks and leaned left and right for an opening in the crowd. Older children perched on the wall above like a row of pigeons. Across the alley, neighbors from the building next door hung from their windows. Everywhere you looked you could see people straining and shifting to see him, but when he raised his hand the entire audience stopped moving. Everyone was silent. Even the children were still. We were watching a sensation.

Another wisp of smoke rose involuntarily from his nostrils. He winced. The old man seemed more like a prophet than a magician and appeared frail in his white coat and turban, until our eyes met. Then he did not look frail. He stared at me as if to say, "You want to see magic? *This* is magic." He raised his head back and up and inhaled a great quantity of air. For a moment, everything in the world stopped moving. I could hear my own heartbeat. Then the magician exhaled and there was fire everywhere. One, two, three flashes of flame from the old man's mouth, bright, hot, and painful. I felt as if I had stepped into the pages of a story. It didn't look like a conjuror's trick or a sideshow stunt from the circus. It looked like magic.

For a moment, the audience was transfixed—stunned, reeling—and then there was a great deal of shouting. The children jumped and squealed and turned to one another, laughing and surprised, but the loudest reaction came from the adults. Behind me I heard Amit booming "Oh! Oh wow!" I could not stop laughing. The man was a street performer and this was ostensibly meant as entertainment but there was nothing trivial about it—fear and joy mixed and taken straight back, all at once, so you felt you were going to fall over. The magician stood there looking at us. The ferocity was gone now, and he didn't look like an old man anymore. He looked like a ten-year-old, eyes bright and full of wonder.

One after another the street magicians of Shadipur Depot performed the feats they have perfected and preserved from generation to generation. When Ishamudin's father did their version of the needle illusion he used no thread, no needles and, as far as I could tell, no illusion. His mouth was empty— unassailably empty—I know how this sort of thing works—and then he closed his eyes and regurgitated mouthful after mouthful of needle-sharp thorns, three inches long. They kept coming, and each time he proved their sharpness by taking one of the thorns and sticking it deliberately into the palm of his hand. By the end, his hand looked like a pincushion and a pile of thorns rested on the ground at his feet. I was beside myself.

I saw rope magic, and water produced from an empty bowl, and then Ishamudin's son Altamas took the stage and together they performed the resurrection illusion. The crowd had grown considerably since the start of the performance, and when they finished, the entire neighborhood broke out into applause.

"Are you glad you came?" Altamas asked as the magicians packed up their equipment and the party moved back down-stairs for a feast, and I said that I was. He was ten or eleven, I think, and spoke flawless English. Like all of the children I had met in this extended family, he treated Andy, Amit, and me with impeccable courtesy and kindness. The contrast between this modern, educated, articulate boy and the ruin of his surroundings was hard to understand. As he helped pack away the props, a rubber cobra fell from a basket, and he noticed as I flinched and stepped backward.

"You are afraid of snakes?" he asked, picking it up and putting it back in the basket.

I nodded. Altamas peered at me, face tight with concern. "Have you been bitten?"

"No. I'm just afraid of them."

"You have no need to fear," he said. "I have been bitten but I am not afraid." He held up his arm and showed me a scar—two white puncture marks and a twisted line connecting the dots and running three inches toward his elbow. "This is where the cobra's fangs went in," he said, "and this is from the knife to release the poison."

"Wait, you were bitten by a cobra?"

"Oh yes," he said, still concerned, as though my fear of snakes was the most important piece of this conversation.

"And to prevent the poison from reaching the rest of your body you cut it out with a knife?"

He nodded, and two other young boys held up arms with similar scars. "But you have no need to fear," he said again. "It's okay. Also," he said, and looked at me strangely, "this is only a rubber cobra."

Ishamudin led us downstairs where he showed me his computer, glowing incongruously in the darkened room. In 1995 Ishamudin gained some notoriety for creating a working version of the infamous Indian Rope Trick, or at least a variation of it.

His performance was featured on TV networks around the world, and this exposure allowed him to bring his show to Europe and Japan. He used the money from this modest success to wire his home with both electricity and Internet access—a feat far more amazing than any of the magic I had just seen—and children from all over the neighborhood came here to learn. "I learned English by radio and television, but this is better," he said, pointing to the computer. "Here you can learn science and math, too."

"Is there a school?" I asked.

"Yes, there is a school. But we want them also to learn in the home."

Ishamudin went to speak with his wife about dinner. Amit and Andy were still on the roof, and for a moment I sat alone on the floor in Ishamudin's living room.

I thought about how many people must see this slum from the train as it rushes through Shadipur Depot station on the way into the city. It is one slum among many on the way to downtown New Delhi—how many notice it at all? And of those who do look up from their phones or their newspapers and see the crumpled ruins of brick buildings and the burning drifts of garbage, how many know that in this dying neighborhood there lives a family of magicians who endure this ruined place and rise in all ways above it? No one on that train could guess that in one of these buildings a group of young boys and girls huddle around a computer screen in the evenings to learn about biology, and astronomy, and evolution.

And if this unexpected richness hidden just behind the illusion of the mundane is here, it could be anywhere. And if it could be anywhere, then my assumptions about most things are almost certainly inadequate. And because my assumptions govern every decision I make and every judgment I pass and form the fundamental worldview from which every single thought, action, and impulse in my life has originated, then all I know for certain is that I am lost. If lives like that can grow in a place like this, then I know nothing. The thing about certainty is that it only takes a tiny crack to bring it all crashing down. And this is not a tiny crack. This family's existence in the middle of a wasteland is a miracle.

~

AN HOUR AFTER the performance we all sat together in front of a five-course meal prepared by Ishamudin's wife with a hot plate and a one-burner stove. Its aromas, tastes, and sheer abundance drew a firm border between this room and the neighborhood on the other side of the bare concrete walls. Outside, the slum seethed under the late-afternoon sun, agitated and decomposing. Inside, we were somewhere else entirely. Inside we had been transported by the warmth of this hospitality and I was embraced like a returning son, long lost and joyfully recovered. *"You have traveled a long way and are welcome here,"* they seemed to say. *"Eat and share with us. Sit and rest. Today this is your home, too."* Piles of rice, naan, a dark orange curry, and a hot green sauce with paneer, steaming and perfect, rested in the center of our circle, which expanded to accommodate a steady stream of visitors who arrived to join the celebration. Cousins, neighbors, and fellow magicians had heard about the visiting American—the American *magician*—and wanted to see this curiosity from the other side of the world. We had nothing in common except magic, but that was enough. Two young boys quietly advanced a rubber cobra toward me on the ground, watching me for a reaction and hissing to each other like snakes. Tea was served. A single lightbulb hung above us to illuminate the meal, and below it the room hummed with laughter, story, conversation.

During the meal I thought about my original motivations for coming to India. I had been frustrated with magic in America and wanted to see if things were somehow better here—more pure, maybe, or more amazing. I wondered if India would be a place where the figure of the Magician had not fallen so far in the eyes of the public. Instead, I found some of the best magicians in the country struggling to work enough to stave off destitution and living in a slum with an open sewer.

I asked Ishamudin how his family had come to live in Shadipur Depot.

He told me about the Indian government's unsuccessful effort in the 1970s to change the world's perception of India as a Land of Mystery that led to a crackdown on street performing and crushed the financial stability of the tribe. Faced with the choice between pursuing modern employment wherever they could find it and staying together in an effort to keep their tradition alive and their family close, the tribe chose the latter and settled in the slum of Shadipur Depot. I asked if he could still make a living on the street in the way his family had done for the last three millennia. He shook his head and told me that most of his income comes from performing at corporate parties, festivals, or private events, and even these are hard to come by. His next show was for a birthday party in the basement of a local McDonald's.

★ ★ ★

I HAD LEFT my bag on the patio, and after the meal Ishamudin walked with me to the roof to find it.

"What do you think of India?" he asked.

"I think that any answer I give will be inadequate. I love it here, but I don't understand it."

"This is essential for love, is it not?" he replied.

"To not understand?"

"No," he said. "To not assume you understand."

We sat.

"Do you believe in real magic?" It took me a full minute to work up the courage to ask the question.

He looked at me sharply, and then, realizing I was serious, his face softened. He looked at the ground, and when he finally spoke, the words came out slowly and carefully.

"I believe in the magic of knowledge. The magic of experience. The magic of learning. The magic of meeting different people. Everything is magic."

He paused for a moment.

"The real magic is your hard work. If you do hard work, that will show you magic. If you are lazy, there will be no magic."

"What's the most amazing thing you've ever seen?" I asked.

"Once in my life I looked at the sky with a telescope. And I felt the air come out of my breath as I saw the stars—the constellations and the Milky Way. I looked at the sky and I thought, 'That is magic.'"

THE TRAIN TO JODHPUR

THE NIGHT WE returned from Shadipur Depot I stayed up late, stretched out on my bed in the guesthouse with the notebook writing everything I could remember about that day. I wrote about the fear, the poverty, the open sewers and the smell of filth. I wrote about Ishamudin and his family. I wrote about the fire breathing. For a few hours I did nothing but write— trying to preserve everything so I could take it home with me. When I was done I flipped through the notebook all the way back to the beginning in Kolkata. I had almost filled it. On the first page I found the question I had written in the train station: *Where do you find wonder?*

Here in India, every moment brought the possibility of discovery, and even as I lay there in the guesthouse I could hear the sounds of the city coming in through the window and the warmth of a breeze that did not feel anything like Iowa. I was awake, and alive, and I didn't want to stop searching. I had come to India to find magic and I had found it, but I realized that it wasn't any one particular moment; it was the process of seeking it that gave these days their sense of impending revelation. It's one thing to find wonder on the other side of the world. But how do you bring it home?

I lay there for a while and then opened the notebook again.

Life in the world is hard. For some more than others, but for all of us more than we admit, and we deploy different strategies to protect ourselves from this hardness. We make our world smaller so we can control it. We make our world simpler so we can understand it. And we reduce ourselves to this diminished scale so we don't accidentally stray outside this fictionalized world and see the danger—but also the majesty—lurking just beyond the borders of our certainty. The result is a world and a life largely free from surprise and uncertainty, but also free from seeing things the way they really are. This, at least, is how it is for me. But the danger is that over time we come to see this pale, anemic version of life as the real thing. We feel the weight of the world but not the wonder, and in time we resign ourselves to one and forget the other.

Once in a while, we remember.

Once in a while something happens—and I have become convinced that it absolutely does not matter what—and we see the cracks in our convictions, and through them a sliver of that larger, wider world outside the one we have constructed. The vision we see there either assaults our sense of control and sovereignty and drives us cowering backward to the world of our making, or it exposes that world for the illusion it really is and invites us upward and onward toward the real thing.

So if your goal is to bring wonder back into your ordinary daily life, start by recognizing that it's not ordinary if you don't want it to be, that it never has been ordinary even if you do want it to be, and that the whole world waits for you to open your eyes and look around you and really see it.

But knowing this theoretically and feeling the vitality of it in your bones are two very different things. Everyone is different, and what strikes one person as awesome and wonderful can be obvious and dull for someone else—magicians learn this very early, unfortunately—so consider the following nothing more than a set of starting points that have been useful for me.

First, think for a moment about the plain fact of the universe's existence. It's a mystery that turns you inside out if you let it. We've learned an enormous amount about how the universe exploded into being from an infinitesimally small point, but nothing at all about how that point came to be in the first place. The jump from nothing to something just before everything exploded into being is unfathomable. Resist the temptation to leave the big questions to other people. They belong to you, too.

Next, follow the Big Bang in your imagination from the time of the explosion all the way to the present moment and see if you can figure out where in that process the particles and atoms bouncing around and sticking to each other according to the laws of the universe acquired the ability to act on their own. For most of that time they were only *reacting*—hurtling through space, joining with other bits of matter—all in accordance to the governing limitations of physics and chemistry. And then at some point you arrived, capable of making your own decisions and living a life of action rather than reaction. How did you jump off the rails? In his Baroque Cycle, author Neal Stephenson described the issue of free will as one of the great labyrinths into which the human mind can lose itself, and even twenty minutes of trying to wrap your mind around the problem is enough to get you thoroughly lost.

Find a sunset, or a sunrise. Go to the ocean, or the Grand Canyon, or a field outside your small town in Iowa at night when the stars are out. Find a way to shift your perspective from the immediate to the infinite, from the very small to the very large. Or go the other way. Watch a raindrop slide down a window-pane and realize this drop of water contains more atoms than there are stars in the universe, and that each of those atoms contains enough power to run a city, or destroy it. Everywhere, all around us, just beneath the surface, hide a complexity and a depth that stagger the imagination. Nothing dissolves the ridic-ulous assumption that we are at the center of the universe like exposure to the actual universe.

There's a fundamental link between wonder and humility. Many of the places people often find wonder—thunderstorms, oceans, the night sky—are also described as "humbling," and though this word has come to have a negative connotation, it shouldn't. Recognizing that we are very small is nothing more than acknowledging the obvious, and any attempt at posturing or pretending we are not is just another part of that fictional, self-created world we're trying so hard to take down.

Now, look at the next person you meet. Recall that even the people who know you the best are aware of only a small frac-tion of the world within you and that most of your inner life—hopes, fears, anxieties, the midnight walk through a snowy winter forest you imagine each night to lull your racing, anxious brain to sleep—most of this is totally unknown to the people in your life. Recognize in the stranger before you this same unknowable universe, and try to find in the awareness of this universe the same sense of infinity and eternity you see in the sky at night.

If you can, do something unexpectedly kind for this stranger. The dinner prepared by Ishamudin's family during my visit to Shadipur Depot and the overflowing hospitality they showed me created one of the most staggering moments of the trip. That evening absolutely knocked me down, but it shouldn't have. Magicians have known for ages that one of the best ways to feel wonder yourself is to give it to someone else. It's like love in that way. You don't sneak into your child's room late at night and secretly swap the hard-won tooth under their pillow for a coin because you want your children to believe in the Tooth Fairy—you do it to give them the experience of magic. It's about enchanting them rather than deceiving them, and you can do that anywhere. Once on tour I was in a diner and saw a woman leave an extraordinarily large tip for one of the wait-resses. I never found out how much, but when the waitress went to clear the table she looked at the receipt, stopped, slowly put the plates back down, and covered her face with her hands. "Oh my god. Oh my god. Oh my *god*!!!" It was like watching someone at a magic show. The waitress grabbed the receipt and ran into the kitchen, laughing and crying. If there is such a thing as real, actual magic in this world, surely this is how it works—us, here, creating it for one another.

Finally, consider yourself. Lie on the ground alone at night and look up at the sky and reflect that everyone you've ever known and everywhere you've ever been is somewhere behind you; that between your spot there on the edge of the world and the depths of the universe before you, you are the only one who can think, learn, hope, dream, and wonder. That power—greater than all of the astronomical distance above—exists in you. "Go within," the tantric yogi in Varanasi had said. "Magical things await."

~

I GOT UP and left the room. The guesthouse had a courtyard filled with plants and a gorgeous square of Indian sky. The stars were washed away by the city light, but you could still see the moon.

I had brought a pay-by-the-minute international cell phone on the trip for emergencies—before leaving I had visions of getting bitten by a cobra and calling Katharine in my last minutes on earth to apologize for everything. Short of that, I was reluctant to use it, as if this trip wouldn't count as a real adventure if I could just call home. Sometimes the world feels too small, and you want it to be bigger.

I punched Katharine's number into the phone and then canceled it and sat there for a minute. Then I called.

"Hello?"

I'm sure the number on her phone had come up as unlisted.

"Hi, Katharine."

My own voice echoed back to me half a second after speaking. The connection was strained and distant, like speaking down a laundry chute.

"Oh my god," she whispered. "How are you? I mean, I'm so glad to hear from you. Are you okay?"

And then, all I wanted to do was go home. "Yes, I am okay. I'm glad to hear your voice."

"You, too, Nate."

Where do I begin?

"Katharine, I met the most remarkable people this afternoon," I said, after about two dollars' worth of silence, and tried to tell her about the street magicians of Shadipur Depot—their life in the slum, their magic, the feast they had cooked for us and the stories they told. I told her about the aarti ceremony in Haridwar and the afternoon in the ashram, and the one-armed monkey who chased me down the alley.

"Are they mean?" she asked.

"Monkeys? Oh god, yes. They're awful."

Another long silence. An entire conversation of pauses and silence.

"Nate, I don't know how to respond. I'm so glad to hear you're okay."

We spoke about her days at home. She told me about our friends and our families, but mostly I was just glad to hear her talk. I wanted to be there immediately.

"When are you coming home?" she asked. "Are you, I mean, are you finished?"

This was a good question.

What are you doing here? I thought. *What do you want?*

It's a terrible question to answer honestly. In a moment of autodidactic ambition I had brought Kierkegaard's *Purity of Heart Is to Will One Thing* on the trip and had fallen out with it almost immediately. I want, distinctly, two things. Ever since meeting Katharine I have harbored a hope of someday moving with her to the country, buying a farm, and leaving it only to restock the cellar with wine and good food, and even then only rarely. Or forget the farm and the wine. A cheap apartment, a hovel, a box—I want to be home with my family.

The other is to be a magician—a great magician—and to chase the experience of wonder and magic through the theaters and venues of America, Europe, the distant mountains of India, or anywhere else the hunt might lead, hurling myself forward from plane to plane and show to show, driving through the night, always searching. I am Captain Ahab. I am Don Quixote. On one window in my studio I have a picture of the raven in flight—an ancient symbol of the magician and a recognition of the necessity of leaving home and going out into the world. On the other I have a picture of a flower. It looks like the rose window from a cathedral. Katharine drew it, and it's a reminder of home and family and all I leave behind when I go on tour. The rose and the raven. The home and the hunt. To hell with Kierkegaard. I want two things.

"I don't know, Katharine. I can't wait to come home. I just—I want to see this through to the end."

"I miss you, Nate."

"I miss you, too."

~

ANDY KNEW THE owner of a hostel in Jodhpur with a rooftop patio and a stock of good Irish whiskey, and this was as good a reason as any to leave New Delhi and spend a few days in the middle of the Rajasthan desert.

The train station in New Delhi is both brighter and better organized than the inhuman citadel in Kolkata and the next night we found our platform with five minutes to spare. Even at ten o'clock the station was filled with people coming and going, and all around our train, passengers hurried to find their cars, load their baggage, and get on board.

An announcement called for us to board the train, and I moved toward the door.

"Nate," Andy said, looking around, "stay here. I'll be right back." He dropped his backpack at my feet, crossed the platform, and disappeared.

I couldn't believe it. I stood there as everyone else filed onto the train. After a moment, I was the only one remaining. I looked at the clock on the wall. Three minutes since Andy left. Less than one minute until our train's departure. At the other end of the platform I could hear the sound of the engine change. The door behind me stood open, but I could see a railway official walking down the platform checking the others.

Andy came racing down the platform at a flat-out run, holding a paper bag. "Pepsi and fried chicken!" he said as he picked up his pack and we boarded the train. We sat on the bench as the train pulled from the station and I watched out the window as the lights of New Delhi and the outlying suburbs slid away into the night.

~

I COULDN'T STOP thinking about Shadipur Depot. Those children have faced hardships I have never even dreamed. They will face them again and again. Their lives will be difficult, and some of them will be short, and by their very existence those children expose my whining about jet lag and the challenges of flying around the world to live out my dream as the crass sort of privileged navel-gazing it is. There's no doubt at all—they have it bad, and I do not.

But I thought about the toddler carrying the baby down the narrow alley and lifting him over the running sewer. He had looked at me as he approached, but it was not a look of suffering. It was a look of pride: *Here, stranger—look at my wonderful baby brother. See how carefully I carry him? See how big I have become, to take on such an awesome task as this? See how my mother trusts me?* I remembered how the children of Shadipur Depot gathered at Ishamudin's home to learn and grow beyond the world of their birth. They felt hope and pride despite their circumstances. It would be easy to pity them, but I had only been there for an afternoon and knew nothing of their inner lives. I didn't want to label them as victims without their participation. It is a kind of arrogance to assume you know more about someone—or something, or everything—than you do. It leads you to act in ways you wouldn't if you better understood your own ignorance.

Earlier I wrote about the way a moment of wonder forces you to expand your understanding of the world, and I think Shadipur Depot stretched mine so completely that it may never return to its former shape. The young boy carrying his brother, the old man who could breathe fire, the family of magicians making a life in the worst neighborhood I'd ever seen—all were so far removed from my previous experience that I couldn't hold them together without letting go of everything else. If a new perspective is wide enough it reduces the scope of your existing knowledge to essentially nothing, and the perspective I gained that day was far wider, and far greater, than anything I had known before. I understood more about everything before I went to Shadipur Depot. Now I don't know.

Amit had spoken about magic tricks as a way to encounter— and then reconcile one's self with—the unknown. He had dropped us off at the train station that evening, and as a parting gift he gave me a copy of a poem he had written about magic— "A rough draft," he had said. "Just a sketch of a poem, really." I

opened my notebook and unfolded the paper he'd given me.
Three lines stood out.

Bless the magician for knowing something I don't.
The appearance and disappearance of the artifacts of this material
world give me an island moment of unknowing,
A mystery that gives me relief from the consuming need to question
everything, and then to answer it.

I read it over and over before folding the poem and tucking it
back into the notebook. Our train car was brightly lit, and the
window reflected the interior of the car, and all I could see was
myself sitting there, trying to look outside.

∼

A DAY LATER Andy and I were installed in red plastic lawn chairs
on the roof of a hostel in Jodhpur watching as the setting sun
turned the brown, orange, and blue of the city below into gold.

Andy held a map of the world spread open on a table,
studying his options.

"What's left?" I asked.

"What do you mean?"

"I mean, you've done everything. You've been everywhere.
What's the next terrifying leap?"

"Going back," Andy said. "Someday."

A breeze had come up at some point, warm and dry, and you
could smell the desert blowing in from just beyond the edges of
town. Andy got up and came back with a beer for each of us.
"I'm going to Hong Kong next. Do you want to come?"

"What's in Hong Kong?"

"I know an artist there. He's an eccentric old man who did very well in business when he was young and now lives in a house by the sea. He paints and rows around the harbor in a little wooden boat. We met there when I first stayed in Hong Kong and he said I should come back anytime."

Andy and I sat in silence. I saw how it all could happen—how I could go to Hong Kong, and then south, maybe, through Indonesia and New Guinea and then on to South America. I'd read about the shamans of the Amazon—maybe I could persuade them to take me in for a month, or a year, and learn the secret language of the birds and the age-old intercessions between the magicians and the wider world. Or I could go west, through southeast Asia, on my way to Kathmandu and the mountain monasteries of Nepal, where I would rise early each morning to watch the sun climb over the Himalayas and then move on to China, by motorcycle, probably, and then up through Mongolia to Russia. Everywhere on the planet was just one decision away.

"Will you stay in Hong Kong for a while?" I asked.

Andy shrugged. "I want to look at all this footage I've been shooting on our trip. Maybe a documentary there."

"You're going to show the whole world that moment when I ran away from the cobra, aren't you?"

"Probably," he said. "You want to come?"

I thought of Katharine. I thought of my job as a magician—I could probably make it back in time to book a good fall tour. I thought of friends and family and all the things you leave behind to travel the world like a vagabond. But—

"Nate?" Andy said again. "What do you think? Want to come to Hong Kong?"

"Yes."

HERE IS REAL MAGIC

I STILL DREAM ABOUT India.

I dream about the wide-open days in Varanasi by the river, and the morning on the banks of the Ganges in Rishikesh when the sun came over the mountains and everything turned to gold. I can close my eyes and see the snake charmer's cobra drop from the basket and come straight for me, and it still raises the hair on the back of my neck. I remember the moment just before the old man performed his fire breathing illusion, when I said to myself *I have been doing this a long time, I know how this shit works, but if he does what I think he is about to do then I don't know anything at all.* And then he did it. The fear, the hope, the allure, the confusion—it's all there, intact, raw, close to the surface. I don't think I've had a day since my return when I haven't thought about my time on the other side of the world looking for magic. The stars over the desert, the child toddling down the alley in Shadipur Depot holding his baby brother tightly in his arms, the candles on the water in Haridwar drifting through the night like falling stars in a meteor shower—bright burning streaks of light you can still see after your eyes are closed. The world didn't fit very well when I came back to Iowa. It still doesn't.

Andy stayed in Hong Kong for a while. From there, he went to the Philippines, then to Australia, then to New Zealand, and then he got hired on as the private chef on someone's yacht and disappeared again. When he resurfaced and returned to the United States a year or so later, he lived on my couch in Iowa City for two months and sold the TV rights to his footage from our trip in India to a television network. The project took off immediately, then languished, then died, and a few clips now live on the Internet as a strange video snapshot of the moments in the trip when we had the camera rolling. I stay up sometimes and watch them, trying to get back to that world, but it's strange seeing it on a screen, safely contained, sterile and remote. You can't feel the heat, or the fear, or the hope.

Since returning from India my advice to anyone and everyone who has asked about my time in that country has been simple: You should go. Go now. Do whatever you need to do to get there. Quit your job, sell your car, leave school, go. Maybe you're like me—you grew up in the States and have done some traveling, and you feel that you have seen a thing or two. India will devour you. You will find kindness, cruelty, poverty, wealth, generosity, heat, noise, dust, and a sea of humanity that will shake your certainties and convictions until they fall out or die along the way. At the end you will stumble, besotted and reborn, from the airplane that brought you home and wonder how and when you can do it all again.

～

ON THE FLIGHT into Hong Kong they served the most elaborate coach-class in-flight meal I have ever encountered before or since—complete with predinner cocktail, salad, predinner wine, dinner, dinner wine, dessert, and a postdinner cocktail. All of this made my entry into the city something of a blur. As we descended, I could see the skyscrapers glowing and flickering with neon-colored LED screens, lighting the clouds from below and turning the night to a Day-Glo haze of pink, yellow, and blue. It was like stepping inside the Internet. I left the plane and immediately fell into an arterial route of moving sidewalks and escalators that whisked me through customs, onto a train, into the city, off the train, onto another train, and then out into the night on a street far from the city center, which now glowed like a video game on the horizon across the water. Here the air was warm and smelled like the ocean, and we walked down the street to the home of the mysterious Uncle Ray.

Since leaving Iowa I had met magicians, snake charmers, con men, holy men, mystics, gurus, street performers, street kids, rickshaw drivers, a poet laureate, and a film producer who traveled everywhere by oversized white Escalade, so ending the trip as the guest of an eccentric millionaire from Hong Kong didn't strike me as particularly unusual. Uncle Ray greeted us at the door, pivoting on the heel of his cowboy boot as he led us down the hallway into his home. He was somewhere between sixty and eighty and looked like Bob Dylan or Captain Jack Sparrow. He welcomed us warmly and showed us to his table where a late dinner and tea service sat waiting.

Uncle Ray had built his home by himself, brick by brick, as a hobby while he still worked in the city. He had laid the bricks about as well as you or I would lay them if given a board of mortar and a stack of bricks—which is to say, poorly—and so his house embodied the uncommon union of haphazard amateurism and unapologetic luxury. I never learned whether he had made his fortune in business or as an artist, but what he lacked in craftsmanship he made up for in vision, and his home was a masterpiece. He'd draped it casually along the rocks leading down from the road to the coast, stopping here for a swimming pool and there for a hot tub, uniting it all with a series of concrete steps poured and shaped by hand.

On the first day I slept—thoroughly, unapologetically, completely. I had a basement room with a floor-to-ceiling window looking out on the ocean, and when I wasn't sleeping I sat on the floor and stared out at the sea, thinking, remembering, trying to decide if any of this was real. I read. I wrote. I went down to the edge of the water and took Uncle Ray's boat out into the harbor.

That evening at dinner I agreed to give a performance for some business acquaintances of Uncle Ray at a private club in downtown Hong Kong, so on the second day I traveled into the city and up the elevator of a midrise tower to a well-appointed lounge with overstuffed furniture and large plate-glass windows looking out on the forest of skyscrapers. I wore my blue T-shirt and hiking pants and felt out of place in the roomful of suits. Twenty or thirty people had arrived for the performance and they clapped politely as I walked to the center of the room. Then silence.

"Thank you. I've been backpacking across India, so please forgive my informal clothing."

Nothing. No response.

"My name is Nate Staniforth. I'm a magician, and I'd like to share a few pieces of magic with you."

It was as if they had been paid to sit as still as possible. No one moved. No one even made eye contact. I felt as though I was speaking to the skyline just beyond their rigid, lifeless bodies.

I thought of the show at Marquette that precipitated this whole adventure, and the way I had felt onstage during the show—numb, mostly, and, if you had pressed me, disillusioned. Since then I had thought a great deal about wonder and bringing it home to my daily life. But as I looked out at the audience I considered that this was my daily life. I was a magician. At some point in India I had realized that I would always be a magician, and magicians do shows—full shows, not just tricks for people I meet during my travels. If I wanted to bring the ideas and experiences from India back with me, I had to find a way for them to live here, too.

Over the next half an hour I threw myself at the audience again and again, urging, prodding, cajoling, provoking, trying to break through and shatter the heavy, stultified formality of this early evening cocktail reception. Magic, urgency, intensity, charm—I tried to light myself on fire, giving everything, as if this one performance would determine the future of my entire life. The audience sat, unmoving and expressionless at first, and then bemused, and then slowly, slowly I could feel them coming to life. One woman in her midfifties held a playing card in her hand, and when she opened it to find that her two of hearts had changed to an ace she stifled a shout, then a smile, and then she didn't try to stifle it anymore. She stood in front of everyone, beaming, and the entire room changed. I stood on a chair in the middle of the room and gathered the audience around me, asking them to leave their seats and come closer. Again, reticence. Hesitation. I started doing magic for them—directly, in their hands, right in front of them. They moved in, gradually, straining for a better view. I did the rubber band trick, the coin vanish, the thread trick, and by the end they had pushed the furniture out of the way so they could all see. We stood there, tied around the chair like a knot, and I ended the show.

"Good night," I said. "Thank you."

Outside, the sun was setting and the entire city glowed brightly with neon light. Inside, everyone milled around drinking white wine and circling the hors d'oeuvres table. In the corner a group of men were studying an envelope I'd used during the show, holding it up to the light, examining the glue that held the edges together, looking for a clue. During the envelope trick in the show they had watched joyfully, amazed, but all of that had gone and they slowly peeled the envelope apart, looking for the secret.

"What are you looking for?" I asked when they noticed me standing nearby. One of them began to explain his theories about the working of the illusion, and I listened for a few moments as he speculated. Magnets. A hidden mirror. Something attached to the back of my hand. Over his shoulder out the window I saw a jet lifting into the sky, heading east. The man watched my face for any clue or sign of agreement, but my attention was wavering. I thought of the candles on the Ganges. I thought of the train ride to Varanasi when the entire trip stretched out before me and the promise of something hidden and wonderful lay somewhere ahead, just out of reach.

"Sir?" the man holding the envelope asked, and I realized he was waiting for a response.

"I'm sorry," I said, "would you excuse me for just a moment? I'll be right back."

I walked to the window. The colors of the city reflected off the water in the harbor—orange, blue, red, green—and the helicopters glowed with red running lights as they darted above the surface like fireflies, muddling the distinction between land and sea and sky. Hong Kong felt wild and unknowable, and for a moment I just stood there and looked at it.

During the five weeks we traveled together, Andy and I had only one real disagreement. It happened an hour or so before flying from Mumbai to Hong Kong, when we stood on Juju beach as the sun dropped toward the horizon. Andy had wanted to film me saying something conclusive about the trip.

"Just say something like 'I came to India to search for magic and learned that real magic is all around you,'" he said.

That was true, but I thought it was a terrible line and told him so.

"Well, say anything. We just need to wrap it up and the sun's going down. You just backpacked across an entire country. What did you learn?"

I didn't know what to say.

But here's my answer to Andy's question. I think you have to grow up twice. The first time happens automatically. Everyone passes from childhood to adulthood, and this transition is marked as much by the moment when the weight of the world overshadows the wonder of the world as it is by the passage of years. Usually you don't get to choose when it happens. But if this triumph of weight over wonder marks the first passage into adulthood, the second is a rediscovery of that wonder despite sickness, evil, fear, sadness, suffering—despite everything. And this second passage doesn't just happen on its own. It's a choice, not an inevitability. It's something you have to deliberately go

out to find, and value, and protect. And you can't just do it
once and keep it forever. You have to keep looking.

THE NEXT DAY I flew home.

I don't remember the flight. My only memory of that day is
of Katharine waiting for me at the arrivals gate, sitting at first
and then both of us running. We were so glad to see each other
that she forgot where she parked the car. We spent forty-five
minutes walking through the parking garage, checking level
after level until we found the car and drove home.

I'M WRITING THE last pages of this book in a hotel room in
Omaha, seven years after returning from India. In forty-five
minutes I'll drive to the theater, and tonight three hundred
people are coming to see the show. I just got off the phone with
Katharine—home with our two young boys, who still don't
understand exactly what I do for a living. "Magic," the two-
year-old says, but we talk about the sky, the clouds, the rain,
and the new shoots of green in his little garden in the back yard
as *magic*, too, so I'm sure he has some confusion about what a
magic show actually entails.

The other day we had a rainstorm and he and I put on our
raincoats and stomped around the puddles in the neighborhood. "A puddle repeats infinity and is full of light," I read
somewhere—Chesterton, I think—"nevertheless, if analyzed
objectively, a puddle is a piece of dirty water spread very thin
on mud."

We walked down the street, splashing in the pools of light,
soaking our clothes and our shoes. He looked at me, his blue

eyes burning brightly, as though we were committing some great and wonderful crime. *Remember this if you can*, I thought. All around us everything was wet, reflective, sparkling in the sun, a world set on fire for a moment.

HERE IS KNOWLEDGE. *The rest is mystery. There is so much yet to be discovered.*

ACKNOWLEDGMENTS

This book started with a declaration—*To the Magicians*, and I'll get to them in a minute—but anyone who has made it this far knows this book could only truly be *dedicated* to one person. Dreams are heavy, and you never carry them alone, and Katharine has somehow managed to help me hold on to mine while simultaneously advancing her own career and holding our household together while I'm away on tour or holed up downstairs writing. In the eleven years we have been married she has been a supporter, collaborator, secret assistant, co-conspirator, companion, and best friend. Katharine, for all of that and for everything still to come, thank you.

This book would not have been possible without the support of many people. I would like to thank my literary agent, Stephen Barr, for championing this book when it was nothing more than an eight-page, single-spaced manifesto, and for ushering it so skillfully through the publishing world. Stephen and I had a number of marathon-length conversations at various stages in the writing process and his ideas and suggestions have been invaluable.

I would like to thank Lea Beresford, my editor, for her generous guidance at every step in this process. Working with a first-time author who is simultaneously writing the manuscript and touring as a magician takes a special kind of patience, and over the past two years Lea has created an ideal environment for this book to grow. Thanks also to the team at Bloomsbury that has worked so hard to give this book a place in the world—specifically, Sara Kitchen, Lauren Hill, Laura Keefe, and Nicole Jarvis. Thank you to Patti Ratchford and Katya Mezhibovskaya for the incredible cover design, and to Emily DeHuff for her careful copyedit of the manuscript.

I would like to thank my manager, Brian Schwartz, Rachel Miller, Arielle Rubin, and the whole crew at 7S, as well as my college booking agent Kate Magill and longtime collaborators Maher Jafari and Chuck Peters.

Thanks to Andy Stoll, not only for years of friendship and collaboration but also for coming with me to India and submitting to the ordeal of becoming a book character.

The magic world is a small, deeply loyal community and I'm honored to be a part of it. There are hundreds of world-class magicians around the globe whom I've never had the chance to meet but whom I think of as allies or brothers and sisters in arms in the struggle to create and perform good magic. Over the past twenty-five years your work has inspired, challenged, provoked, and flat-out astonished me. I love magic more than just about anything, and if you do too, thank you.

I've had the opportunity to work with a number of magicians who have shaped my understanding of the craft for the better.

Special thanks to friends and collaborators Brian Brushwood, Daniel Martin, Wayne Houchin, Gus Davis, CJ Johnson, Peter Boie, Norman Ng, Jonny Zavant, Chris Carter, Justin Flom, Justin Willman, James Galea, Blake Vogt, and Brent Braun.

Additionally, the published works of Derren Brown, David Berglas, David Britland, Juan Tamariz, Darwin Ortiz, Teller, Barrie Richardson, Sam Sharpe, Tommy Wonder, Stephen Minch, Michael Ammar, Arturo Ascanio, Jamy Ian Swiss, Eric Mead, Paul Harris, Max Maven, Eugene Burger, Robert Neale, Jim Steinmeyer, Richard Kaufman, John Cassidy, and Anthony Owen have been essential to my own thinking about magic. Thank you.

I am not an anthropologist, and while I have gleaned personal insight from the writing of David Abram and Bronislaw Malinowski, the interpretation of their works in this book is mine alone. Please do not hold them accountable for any misunderstanding on my part. The interview with David Abram referenced in this book comes from a conversation with writer Scott London.

I'd like to thank my parents, Art and Jayne, my brother, Ben, my sister, Kimberly, my in-laws, Martin and Mary Ellen, and my longtime friends Brandon Crase, Jon Sargent, Dave and Renee Gould, and Jay and Ellen Holstein.

Finally, I'd like to thank my two children. Parts of this book were written with each of you sleeping as babies on my lap—helping, we called it—and one day I'm sure you'll both read it. I hope it helps you understand why I had to go away sometimes, and what I was looking for while I was out there. When you're older I hope you remember to look for it, too, in your own way, and I hope more than anything that someday you find it.

A NOTE ON THE AUTHOR

NATE STANIFORTH is a magician, performer, writer, traveler, and former host of Discovery Channel's international hit TV show *Breaking Magic*. For more than a decade, Nate has toured the United States as one of the busiest working magicians in the country and shared the philosophical underpinnings of his work through both a TEDx Talk and a lecture at the world-famous Oxford Union. He lives in Iowa City.

www.natestaniforth.com